Note for Librarians: A cataloguing record for this book is available from Library and Archives Canada at www.collectionscanada.ca/amicus/index-e.html

ISBN: 978-1-4120-8784-1 (sc)
ISBN: 978-1-4251-9636-3 (e)

Printed in the United States of America. Printed on paper with minimum 30% recycled fibre. Trafford's print shop runs on "green energy" from solar, wind and other environmentally-friendly power sources.

Except where indicated, all Scripture quotations are taken from the NEW AMERICAN STANDARD BIBLE, © 1960, 1962, 1963, 1968, 1971, 1972, 1973, 1975, 1977, by the Lockman Foundation. Used by permission.

Scripture quotations marked (AMP) are taken from THE AMPLIFIED BIBLE, Old Testament copyright © 1965, 1987 by the Zondervan Corporation. The Amplified New Testament copyright © 1958, 1987 by the Lockman Foundation. Used by permission.

Scripture quotations marked (NLT) are taken from the Holy Bible, NEW LIVING TRANSLATION, copyright © 1996. Used by permission of Tyndale House Publishers, Inc., Wheaton, Illinois 60189. All rights reserved.

Scripture quotations marked (MSG) are taken from THE MESSAGE. Copyright © 1993, 1994, 1995. Used by permission of NavPress Publishing Group.

Some Images © 2006. www.FaithClipart.com

TRAFFORD
PUBLISHING™
Offices in Canada, USA, Ireland and UK

Book sales for North America and international:
Trafford Publishing, 6E–2333 Government St.,
Victoria, BC V8T 4P4 CANADA
phone 250 383 6864 (toll-free 1 888 232 4444)
fax 250 383 6804; email to orders@trafford.com
Book sales in Europe:
Trafford Publishing (UK) Limited, 9 Park End Street, 2nd Floor
Oxford, UK OX1 1HH UNITED KINGDOM
phone +44 (0)1865 722 113 (local rate 0845 230 9601)
facsimile +44 (0)1865 722 868; info.uk@trafford.com
Order online at:
trafford.com/ 06-0540

10 9 8 7 6 5 4 3 2 1

I give you my WORD

In the beginning was the Word, and the Word was with God, and the Word was God

Jn

I give you My WORD

Barbara A Pavey

www.igiveyoumyword.com

And the Word became flesh,

and dwelt among us

Jn 1:14

WORD

WORD in the bible refers to Jesus Christ, often to the scriptures and the law of God, as well as to spoken or written utterance.

Acknowledgements

This book was a creative concept, a journey, a process. The birthing of a dream. A gift which I present back to God – by using it. Created to accomplish great things!

This space is occupied by a veritable God-given 'cloud of witnesses', who have surrounded me over the years with their support and encouragement. An army of special people who have always urged me to run the race with endurance, to fix my eyes on Jesus, the Author and Finisher of my faith, and to not grow weary or lose heart.

I salute each and every one of these priceless treasures, some of whom are now cheering from glory. Thank you, for enabling me to cross the finishing line of achievement.

Special thanks for their tireless work and patience to Derek Bradbury for the Cover artwork and interior graphics (nu.graphics@yahoo.co.uk) and to Allison Papworth (Allison@toucansurf.com) for layout and editorial services.

Special Dedication

To the memory of the late Reverend Leslie Elliott who always believed in the gift of writing he saw in me, and went out of his way to urge me to use it.

To my husband, mum, dad and brother who have each played such an important and special part in my life.

To Father, Son and Holy Spirit, my triune Rock, and my life.

CONTENTS

WORDSONGS

WORDTHOUGHTS

WORD TO WORD

A WORD IN YOUR EAR

THE SPOKEN WORD

THE LAST WORD

INTRODUCTION

I GIVE YOU MY WORD is full of choices. It is one of those books that can be picked up and put down at leisure. It is a devotional, yet without fixed boundaries.

You may wish to worship the Lord with WORDSONGS (poetry), WORD TO WORD (prayer, confession of His Word back to Him), WORDTHOUGHTS (reflections, jottings, musings) or to join me in WORDSEARCH (bible study).

Variety is the spice of LIFE and the Holy Spirit puts Creator power within us in order that we may explore different avenues during our daily times with Him.

I GIVE YOU MY WORD is a God-inspired title. He gave *us "the Word made flesh"* and the word He speaks is Spirit, Truth and Life.

Be blessed in the use of this book and may it inspire you as you fellowship with the King of Kings and Lord of Lords.

I give you My WORD

In the beginning was the Word, and the Word was with God, and the Word was God

JnF

WORDSEARCH

1

WORDSEARCH

Jesus said in *Jn 6:63* *"the words that I have spoken to you are spirit and are life."* *Heb 4:12* says that the Word of God is able to reach the parts of you that nothing else can. It's a mirror revealing the heart of God. It deals with the real issues that you face and if you embrace the scriptures as a true and trusted friend, you can learn and discern the awesome ways of God and His plan for living life to the full.

This section allows you to give time and place to the study of God's Word so that you can present yourself to God approved, accurately handling the Word of Truth (*2 Tim 2:15 Amp*).

2 Tim 3:16-17 emphasizes that *"all Scripture is inspired by God and profitable for teaching, for reproof, for correction, for training in righteousness; that the man of God may be adequate, equipped for every good work."*

Feed daily on the godly ingredients of the gospels and watch your faith grow.

Use the 'Check It Out' section at the foot of each WORDSEARCH article for further study.

An Audience With… The Holy Spirit

We are living in exciting times. Everything is building up to the soon return of the Lord Jesus Christ and there's a quickening, a stirring, an expectancy in our spirits of something about to happen.

Remember the account of Creation in Genesis chapter one? The earth was void and without form, but the Holy Spirit was there waiting, poised for action and hovering excitedly. He knew something was about to break. He was involved as a part of the Godhead. At the very command of faith the Holy Spirit couldn't contain Himself any longer and burst upon the scene. He's the Executor of the will of God, and carried out each instruction powerfully and meticulously as it was ordered. He released the power of God to bring forth the worlds and everything they were to contain. He set a pattern then and has been consistent in it ever since.

It's almost as though Holy Spirit is poised once again to move on behalf of the Godhead. He is the powerhouse part of the Holy Trinity and He longs for all believers to enter into a close relationship with Him and get to know Him intimately.

Powerful things happen in the lives of those who dare to enter into this kind of fellowship and walk with Him. Awesome experiences of faith await those who honour the presence of the Holy Spirit in their lives.

The book of Acts is a whole catalogue of the exciting power and diversity He brings and the difference He makes to lives. The subject of the Holy Spirit is just so vast, where can we possibly start? He cannot be contained, but that's the very beauty and attraction of Him. He is all and in all.

May these lines simply serve as an introduction to this most wonderful member of the Godhead and of the benefits of cultivating a close intimate relationship with Him. His ultimate aim is to point you in the direction of Jesus and to see His Name and purposes be glorified. How well do you know Him? I mean *really* know Him? He longs for fellowship with us. Do you take time on purpose to sit and wait for Him and enjoy His company and learn from Him? Do you start each day by inviting His presence into your every moment? Do you reverence the holiness of His presence within you? Do you realise that all the fullness of the Godhead dwells within you, waiting to be released? Are you aware that it's the same power that raised Jesus from the dead? The Holy Spirit.

He Who intervenes in the affairs of man, averting disasters, helping you to make right choices and decisions, teaching you the Truth of God, guiding you, bringing to your remembrance the Word when you need to stand on it, convicting you of sin, righteousness and judgement, keeping you on the right path. He Who will alert you to pray for a particular person, ministry, nation or situation, even awake you to do so – it is the Holy Spirit. Often He will stir pray-ers to pray before something happens and later appears in the media by way of confirmation. You'll stand in awe as you recognise that you were instrumental in intervening to intercede on God's behalf.

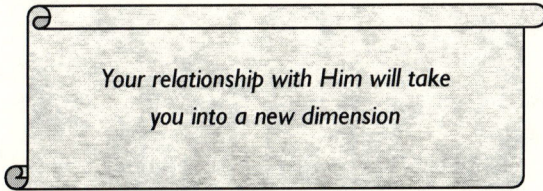

> *Your relationship with Him will take you into a new dimension*

He desires to educate you in the ways of the Spirit. He needs you so charged and fuelled by Him that should it be necessary, He could even transport you across the world to meet a need. Remember Philip and the Ethiopian eunuch? (*Acts 8:26-40*). It's stepping out of the world of the flesh and operating under the instructions and authority of the Holy Spirit, co-working with God.

It is the Holy Spirit Who gives you a heavenly language with which to communicate with God in praise, prayer, prophecy, deliverance.

He takes those words, wraps them in power, translates them into the perfect will of God and presents them to the Father, returning in due time with the answer. He puts creative ideas, strategies, inventions and supernatural abilities and thinking into you.

After all your praying, just linger a while with the Holy Spirit. You'll learn the ways of love from Him. It'll revolutionize your relationships. He also wants to show you great and mighty things that you know not, including the things that are to come. To prepare you, God's Word says that before things happen, you will know them. The gift of knowledge will begin to operate through you.

You'll learn how to be a worshipper from Him. God is looking for those who will worship Him in spirit and in truth. The Holy Spirit is the only One Who can teach you that. We haven't even begun to understand the dimension and power of worship yet. It's the language of heaven. It'll bring the glory of God upon you if you are willing to be taught. Worship will accomplish what nothing else can. I believe the Holy Spirit aches for God's people to catch this revelation.

2 Cor 13:14 talks about *"the grace of the Lord Jesus Christ, and the love of God, and the fellowship of the Holy Spirit."* Our hearts become so quickly hardened that we overlook or fail to be touched by the unconditional forgiveness and sacrificial love of God.

It's the Holy Spirit Who pours all grace and love into our hearts through His communion or fellowship with us. The term means 'communicating and travelling together,' having a companion in life. Always with you, always for you. The challenge is, where do you take Him? What things do you say and do in His Presence? How do you treat others? Is He grieved by your thoughts and actions? Is He restricted or restrained in you by your lack of faith or understanding? Communion, or fellowship, refers to that which forms the basis of friendship. It comes from familiarity that stems from knowing someone's ways and character through investing sufficient time with them to enable that trust and ease. Without Him, you *have* no real spiritual life, no faith, no power, no fervent prayer-life.

The more you think about it, the less you can do or be without the Person of the Holy Spirit operating and flowing freely through you. How hungry *are* you for Him? How strong your desire to know Him? How much freedom has He to make His home in you? This is an unprecedented time in history and the Holy Spirit wants and needs to indwell every part of the Body of Christ to see it moving and operating in the full power, holiness and authority of God, spreading the gospel, growing up into Christ, standing as His Bride longing for His return so that the reign and Kingdom of God may be ushered in and the Holy Spirit can complete His work on earth within the Church.

He's here to see that the creative work of Christ overthrows the destructive work of Satan through the spiritual warfare of the saints. How? Every time you walk in love, bring healing, salvation, deliverance, sing praises, worship, use the gifts of the Spirit, pray and walk by faith and in Holy Spirit Fruit, you are destroying the works of the evil one and his demonic cohorts. Every time you refuse to believe a lie, you are tearing down enemy territory. Every time you take your place and call on the Name of Jesus and confess His Word, you are battering and demolishing satanic strongholds and you are doing it through the power of the Holy Spirit. He wants you to depend on Him.

The Bible refers to the Holy Spirit as God. He carries out the work that none but God can do, raising the dead, healing, convicting of sin, bringing salvation, reproving, correcting, training in righteousness. As God, He is eternal, all-knowing, ever present and therefore trustworthy. He never leaves or forsakes you. He is also called the Comforter, the One called alongside to help. He intercedes on our behalf. He testifies of the Lord. He calls people to the work of ministry.

He has feelings and emotions – joy, anger, pleasure, sorrow. He has the intellect to search the deep things of God.

SYMBOLIC NAMES OF THE HOLY SPIRIT

Fire   Light, power, consumes sin, presence of God

Water   Indispensable to life. Cleansing. Refreshing

Wind   Exists everywhere. In continuous motion. Cannot be contained or controlled. Brings freshness. Powerful or gentle

Oil   Anointing. Holy Light. Preservation

Rain   Sustains and brings forth life. Nourishes. Replenishes. Natural cycle. Brings harvest

Dove   Emblem of peace. Meekness. Humility. Easily grieved. Anointing

Wine   Fullness, gladness, rejoicing, boldness, insulator from pain, strength, freedom

Seal   Ownership, authority, guarantee, foretaste of heaven

GIFTS

The Holy Spirit will also impart gifts to enable you to perform all God purposes for and through you. (*1 Cor 12:4, 7-11*). Those gifts are tools not toys, given for works of service. They are not prideful trophies.

FRUIT

The Holy Spirit brings about the necessary changes in your character to make you like Jesus and attract others to Him through you (*Gal 5:22-23*). He'll keep you clean and pure. He's the *Holy* Spirit. Don't get entangled in other things. Stay focussed on Him. Concentrate on spending time with Him.

UNITY

The baptism in the Spirit brings oneness and breaks down every barrier. It is for every believer and joins them all into one Body, Christ's universal Church (*1 Cor 12:13*).

1 John 2:20 says *"you have an anointing from the Holy one, and you all know."* The Holy Spirit leads you into all truth and protects you from deception.

The priests bore the Ark of the Covenant. They carried the Presence of God with them. They still had to put their toes into the water before they experienced the miraculous parting of the River Jordan so that they could cross into new territory. Now, the Presence of God is carried by us in these temples of our body. Earthen vessels containing the glory of God.

You have the potential to step into the power and flow of God's anointing and go places in God, break new ground that maybe you've never dreamt of or imagined previously. To flow in the supernatural as priests and kings of the Lord.

Lk 4:18 "The Spirit of the Lord is upon you, because He has anointed you to preach the gospel to the poor. He has sent you to proclaim release to the captives, and recovery of sight to the blind, to set free those who are distressed, to proclaim the favourable year of the Lord." Dare to open up your heart and life to a relationship with the Holy Spirit that will lead you into the dimension of eternity.

Check it out: Take a peek into the Book of Acts – the Acts of the Holy Spirit

Blessings Of Brokenness

Ps 51:8 – "Make me to hear joy and gladness, let the bones which you have broken rejoice."

There are many instances throughout the Bible of broken lives and hearts. Stories where men and women have gone through personal encounters with God that have left them stripped of their own strength and acutely aware of their mortal frailty. Times when it seemed as though life's bubble had burst, shattering dreams, wrecking ambitions, causing one's world to be torn into pieces and all hope to be lost.

Jesus, at His baptism *(Lk 3:21-22)*, received the blessing of His Father in heaven and the equipping for ministry. However ... He was blessed to be broken. His calling led Him through the wilderness of temptation all the way to the Cross of Calvary, and the brokenness of separation from the Father as Jesus bore the sin of the world upon His shoulders. Yet ... *"for the joy set before Him"*, the joy of birthing the Church and bringing many back to God, *"He endured the Cross with all its shame" (Heb 12:2).*

Jesus came to bind up the broken-hearted *(Lk 4:18)* and the wounds of His own brokenness still bring that healing to others.

David said *(Ps 51:17)* *"a broken and contrite heart You will not despise."*

God breaks the proud to grace the humble. Your scars enhance your beauty.

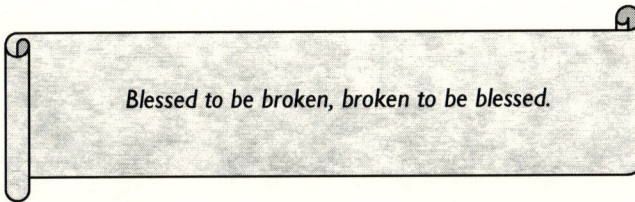

Blessed to be broken, broken to be blessed.

Bring It On!

BACKGROUND

Of all the gospels, John's very much emphasizes the fact that Jesus is God. He sums up everything by saying that the examples quoted of some of the many miracles and deeds performed by Jesus *"have been written that you may believe that Jesus is the Christ, the Son of God; and that believing you may have life in His Name."* (Jn 20:31)

John's approach is to unfold, to present one step at a time, his proof of Jesus' deity – and he's also a listener. This is evidenced in the many times he quotes the things spoken by Jesus, giving more emphasis to the words than the actions. It reveals the close proximity John always maintained to his Lord and the accompanying closeness of the relationship. There are several instances when John was the first to do something or be somewhere, or was seen at Jesus' side, such was the expression of his love for the Master. He was ultimately rewarded with the entrusting to His care of Jesus' earthly mother, and he was the one who had the Revelation of Jesus Christ communicated to him on the Isle of Patmos. I wonder how closely we walk with Jesus and how hungry is our desire for Him?

Are we enjoying the benefits, rewards and revelation that comes from that unique intimacy? John is a good gospel to study as each step is a complete picture in itself and there are some wonderfully majestic truths unfolded throughout the chapters. He is rich in symbolism and the nuggets of treasure to be found are well worth the search. He shows that Jesus used the common things of everyday life as illustrations of deeper spiritual applications. What John is trying to unfold in this gospel is what Jesus coming into the world means to you and I.

THE WEDDING AT CANA

Jn 2:1-11

We read here of the very first miracle or sign that Jesus performed. In verse 43 of Chapter 1 we learn that Jesus *"purposed to go into Galilee"* and now we know why. On the way He made some converts and disciples. Don't overlook any opportunities as you go through your day.

V1-2 On the third day in the events surrounding the launch of Jesus' public ministry, He planned to meet His mother and brothers at a wedding celebration. He was a man of the people, never proud or aloof from them.

He identified with them socially and spiritually, never giving the impression that He was above anyone. In fact He insisted that the source of all goodness was His Father in heaven (*Lk 18:19*).

The new converts accompanied Jesus to the wedding and would be observing all that was going on, all part of their training as they watched His behaviour and example. Our lives are an open book to others – what are we teaching them about godliness?

At the simplest level, the very presence of Jesus was indicating His approval of the sanctity of the marriage relationship, where there was to be a leaving and a cleaving. The leaving of parental ties and the establishing of a new family partnership. Not one thing that Jesus said or did was insignificant, such that John uses the very word 'signs' rather than miracles to portray that the purpose of Jesus' ministry was to establish markers of the Kingdom of God and His deity.

Jesus would be celebrating His own marriage ceremony with His Bride the Church, at the Marriage Feast of the Lamb, the wine outpoured would be the final once-for-all sacrifice of the shedding of the blood by the Lamb of God taking away the sin of the world (*Jn 1:29*). God has always had a special sanctified relationship with His people, first of all being Israel, and then in Christ's relationship with the redeemed church.

V3 We now have a situation which is potentially very degrading for those providing the hospitality, particularly in this culture. Wedding celebrations could last for as long as a week. We're not informed as to why there was a shortage of wine as that is not the important point. The mother of Jesus simply came to Him and laid out the facts. She told Him what the problem was and set the pattern for us to *"cast all our anxiety on Him, because He cares for us"* (*1 Pet 5:7*).

V4 The literal translation is 'dear woman, what business is that of ours?' 'Woman' is a term of endearment here, not an abusive remark. Jesus uses the same expression later on when, hanging upon the Cross, He makes provision for His mother in the entrusting of her into the care of John. John would also receive comfort for his own grief at losing his dearest friend and Saviour.

"My time has not yet come." Scripture says that there is a time and season for everything, yet we already know from this gospel that Jesus was at the beginning of His earthly ministry. His heart and focus was already towards Calvary and beyond and He was indicating that it was not yet His time to pour out His blood. His priority was always greater than the actual miracles He performed, they simply being pointers, or signs that He had come to set free the captives. The emphasis was not on the feat but the Father. How would His mother react to this challenge of her faith?

V5 She proceeds to instruct the waiting servants! The Greek word for servant implies complete dependence upon the master and they would act in obedience to every given instruction. Again Jesus is the Servant of servants. He came to serve, not to be served, a man under authority. The same word for servant is used in *Phil 2:6-11*. Completely given over to the will of His Father. Jesus was given authority to work the works of the Father, and He later was to hand it on to His followers, including you and I who believe (*Mat 28:18*). He taught as one having authority, yet used it with humility.

V6 Again, it's noted here that there were six stone pots deliberately placed for the purpose of religious cleansing, a part of eastern hospitality. *Mark 7* tells us how Jesus felt about such religious ritual and what really matters on the subject of clean or unclean. God clearly looks at the heart rather than what is done for show or ceremony (outward appearances). The religious routines appeared to indicate that anyone could indulge in all sorts of excess as long as they continued to satisfy the legalistic requirements of the day! Perhaps the number six might remind us of works of the flesh which will never satisfy a holy God and will always fall short of spiritual perfection. It will also remind us of the miraculous work of Creation in Genesis, which was performed over six days, before God rested.

Here before everyone stood Jesus, representing godly wholeness and cleanness. Freshly baptised of John, anointed for ministry by the Holy Spirit, He silently proclaimed the fact that it is by repentance of heart and forgiveness of sin that one becomes clean, not by the washing of the body. It's spiritual purification that counts with God. The pots had the potential to hold a great capacity of water and as believers, the same is true of us as the Holy Spirit cleanses, fills and empowers us – for service.

V7 Jesus says *"fill the water pots with water"* and they were filled to the brim. You might say that these verses are brim full of symbolism. If we come empty of ourselves and place ourselves in utmost dependence upon Him, if we come with true repentance and know the forgiveness of our sins by the washing of the Lord Jesus Christ, the Anointed One, then we can know the fullest measure of His indwelling power in our lives through allowing ourselves to be filled with the Holy Spirit.

> *Jesus stood here full of power and He was about to pour it out into the lives of others.*

The water was not to stay in the jars. Something needed to happen to it.

33

V8 Jesus issues a command and the response was simple yet immediate. They obeyed! They were partakers of a miracle as they drew out the water. Something had been created that was not previously there. A 'super' had been added to the natural. Water had become wine. Fruit, or fruitfulness had come, and it was the privilege of the Head Steward, or Wine Waiter, to experience (taste) it.

Now, the same is true in our lives. When we are filled with the water of the Holy Spirit, it is not a luxury we keep for ourselves.

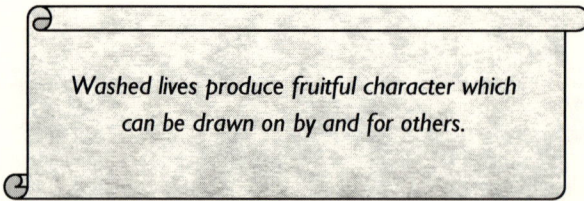

> *Washed lives produce fruitful character which can be drawn on by and for others.*

It should be their privilege to taste and see fruit in our lives. In our dealings with and responses to others, do we pour out love, joy, peace. In other words, do they see Jesus?

This was fermented wine. Strong drink. It had an intoxicating effect. Again symbolic of the fullness and power of the Holy Spirit in our lives. God's word warns us against the effects of drinking intoxicating wine, but instead to be filled with the Spirit (*Eph 5:18*).

The presence of the Holy Spirit in our lives should release us of all inhibitions and have a strong life-changing effect on us and others.

V9 The Head Waiter tasted something that surprised him. Our lives should leave others asking questions, wanting to know more. He had tasted the good, but was now partaking of the best. An encounter with Jesus put everything else into the category of mediocrity and the waiter wanted an explanation.

Have you got a reason to give for the hope that is in you when asked? He called over the bridegroom, the one that was responsible for the feast and the celebration, and in whose honour was the occasion.

Equally, others may be perplexed and puzzled at the grace of God that transforms the weak and the foolish, the nothings and nobodies into the very best that God can produce. The Bridegroom is preparing His Bride for the celebration of celebrations, to take and taste, experience and enjoy for all eternity, because He's purchased her with the highest price – His own blood.

V10 The waiter points out that something has occurred outside of normal procedure and practice.

The choicest wine is usually dispensed first and the cheaper when everyone has had their fill, become drunk and is past noticing or caring! Here the reverse situation was true.

It's like a picture of the first Adam and the last Adam. The first Adam came in the likeness of God and God said that His creation was very good, but sin's corruption and its effect led the human race astray and that goodness ran out. But then, God produced His best! The last Adam, Jesus *said "come to Me, all who are weary and heavy-laden, and I will give you rest" (Mat 11:28) and "blessed are those who hunger and thirst for righteousness for they shall be satisfied" (Mat 5:6).*

He said that those who came thirsty would be satisfied and never thirst again and He was to be poured out as a drink offering for many. (Jn 19:34, 1 Jn 5:6). With God, the best is His final standard.

VII Jesus had now 'come clean.' He'd revealed His power, glory and authority. He'd taken the lid off God. As a bride and groom celebrate their union and look forward to a joyful future together with the fruitfulness of children, so Christ had come to point the way back into oneness with God and in bringing many sons to glory as the first-fruits. He, with us, would know eternal joy and rejoicing.

He'd come to make visible the invisible, to reveal the mystery of God to the world, and to bring God recognition, renown and honour by men again giving Him His rightful place in their lives.

As a result of what they saw and heard at *"this beginning of His signs,"* His disciples put their faith in Jesus. They believed in Him enough to lay down their own lives and follow Him. Does the same apply to us?

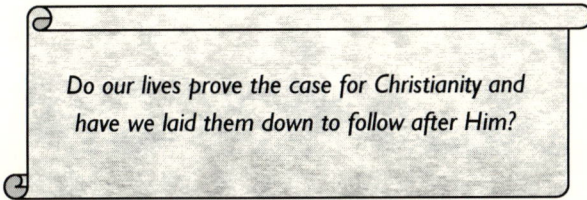

> *Do our lives prove the case for Christianity and have we laid them down to follow after Him?*

This is a familiar passage of scripture to many and it may have been glossed over on many previous occasions as the first of many miracles and so perhaps of little consequence.

It in fact summarised the whole of Jesus' purpose and ministry – to bring others to faith in and restore their relationship with God and so prepare a Bride for the Bridegroom. He came to say *"I AM the true Vine"* (Jn 15:1).

This is an amazing gospel with outstanding insight. Check it out!

Do You See Anything?

Mark 8: 22-26

It happened here that a blind man needed some assistance in being brought to Jesus. From then on, it was a one-on-one encounter. That's the way it is physically, and spiritually. At the end of the day, others can only take you so far. They may bring a measure of enlightenment, they may be of some help, but the highest and noblest course of action is simply to introduce someone to Jesus – and let Him take over.

He took the man and led him out of the village. This man's life had now been touched by a Divine hand. There was a mark of eternity on him. When that happens, lives are never the same again. Jesus brought him out of what may have been a distracting, perhaps faithless or negative environment. It would most certainly have been a familiar and secure one for a blind man! He drew him away from the crowds so that the man could focus his whole attention on Jesus and know that Jesus valued him as an individual. So it is when the Lord would seek our attention.

He has a way of engineering circumstances and leading us away from things perhaps unseen and unknown to us, yet known to Him to be distracting in His purposes for us. Could it be that our secure, familiar comfort-zone lifestyles are limiting, hindering or restricting our potential? The expression 'not seeing further than the end of our noses' springs to mind.

This man now knew that Jesus was singling him out for a specific purpose. Jesus' plan was to do the man good, not to harm him, and to give him hope and a future. To meet his individual needs. One-on-one relationship. It's always God's way. Our first and highest calling is to be with Jesus.

Even so, the man may not have been *quite* prepared for what happened next. Here he was, out of his known environment, vulnerable, in the hands of a complete stranger, who then proceeded to spit upon his eyes! Spitting upon the very source of his discomfort and distress. Adding insult to injury it seemed. Sometimes Jesus touches us just where we are weak and vulnerable. It seems things get worse before they get better.

> *Sometimes there's a sorrow*
> *before there's a suddenly.*

All the man could do was to stand still and trust that this Jesus knew what He was doing and wasn't out to humiliate him further.

What was the significance of this method of approach? Jesus did many unorthodox things. The results are what matters. *(c/f Mk 7:31-35 for similarities)*. Smith Wigglesworth adopted many unusual methods in his ministry – but the results spoke for themselves. Divine healing power was imparted as Jesus lay hands on this man *(see I Tim 4:14)*. Change was taking place in his life.

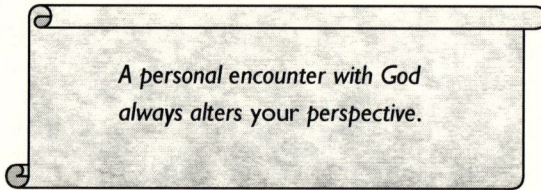

A personal encounter with God
always alters your perspective.

"Do you see anything?" Have you ever wondered why this man only received partial healing at this point? Was it because Jesus made a mistake? Didn't have enough faith or power? Of course that wasn't the case. What then? Could it be that Jesus wanted a faith confession from the man? We're told he 'looked up'. In other words, he gained sight. The man was trying to describe things he may never have seen before and he started out in the flesh. His words though, were building faith which Jesus used to bring about a complete work, restoration of vision and clarity of sight. Faith is progressive.

We walk, not run by faith, but our faith, as it grows stronger, enables us to see the previously unseen and to understand the things of God more clearly and definitely. It's a miracle of grace. He *heard* the word and then he *saw* the Word!

Jesus sent the man home and cautioned him not even to enter the village again. When you meet Jesus face to face and experience first hand His love, His touch, His hand upon your life and your eyes are opened to His truth, you'll not want to return to your old way of life. Even the familiar will lose its attraction. You'll want to walk in a new direction and experience a relationship with Jesus and hear Him say to you – "Do you see anything" as He opens your spiritual eyes and your sight is restored and you see everything clearly.

The man looked intently – with a view to seeing – and he saw.

What about you?

Check it out: Mk 7:31-35, 1 Tim 4:14

For Such A Time As This

Est 4:10-17

This story has it all – male chauvinism, women's lib, feminism, political intrigue, racial prejudice, ethnic minorities, social outcasts. Even a Miss Persia competition! Plus an attempt at ethnic cleansing.

This is one of the stories in the bible where you see the hand of God so clearly, yet the book doesn't refer to God at all. Nonetheless there is the unmistakeable moving of a sovereign power. His influence vibrates dynamically throughout these pages.

The kingdom in question here is not the kingdom of God. It's a secular kingdom. Esther was called to take up her position and play out her role/destiny in what today could be any modern, godless society.

The story is a well-known one, that of a beautiful young Jewish woman caught in a web of circumstances over which she had no personal control.

She was called to make a decision between the demands of her own nation or her self-preservation. Could be the same for any of us.

God has placed us in situations/circumstances/positions 'for such a time as this.' It's no mistake where we are, what we are or when and why we were born. Even if we were unplanned, God knew! God decided to place us into this particular slot in eternity. We each have a destiny to fulfil in our 'kingdom.' Jesus had a particularly sensitive heart towards His women followers, and many of them were society's rejects! He took them, released them from emotional, physical and spiritual bondage, esteemed them, respected them, and drew out from them their full and absolute potential, giving them dignity and standing in His circle. Many of the seemingly insignificant acts of women are treasured and recorded in scripture as a memorial and testimony for us all. Those stories have each their own beauty. In Christ there is neither male nor female for He sees not gender, but availability. He pours out His gifts on all His children, and whom He calls, He equips.

You are here today because the Lord has a divine mission for you to accomplish which could have far-reaching effects on generations to come. Consider that! No Esther, no Nehemiah! God is working an eternal plan and you fit into it precisely, accurately and strategically. Each one has a kingdom of influence in which their presence matters! It may be home, job, family, ministry.....

It took great courage for Esther to take her stand for God at a moment filled with danger. It may not always be easy following God but it's never boring! You too may be a minority of one in the natural but God will take what you give Him and add His super to your natural. He's looking for a channel, not a reservoir.

OUR REASONING

Mordecai became Esther's guardian and mentor, and had to address her excessive reasoning. She had natural concerns for her own welfare. Scripture is so real and honest in showing us the human side of God's eventual heroes and heroines. She needed someone outside of the situation to challenge her thinking. *"Who knows whether you have not come to the kingdom (to royal position) for such a time as this?"* It was a journey, a process, and she had gone through much preparation to reach this point. It's the same with you and me. The royal King, the Lord God, has called us to royal status and much has been sown into our lives to prepare and equip us in His service.

A prepared path, a prepared vessel.

WHAT TIME?

A time when outward appearance mattered more than inward reality. *Chapter 1* opens with a scene of exotic luxury. Sheer decadence and opulence. Grandiose lifestyle. Flamboyant materialism. Boastfulness and pride.

For six months King Ahaseurus held a lavish party, culminating in a gathering of all the nobility and elite, the A-List celebrities, to feast on all his magnificence. Picture the scene - golden drinking goblets, gold and silver couches, marble, fine linens, precious stones, beautiful gardens. An ostentatious display of wealth, prosperity and arrogance. Cosmetic trappings and self-gratification in the extreme! The average designer lifestyle of today. The priority was sensual indulgence, not personal integrity.

Read through the chapters and note the parading of young women before the king. There came a time when Queen Vashti rebelled. Could it be because she tired of the humiliation and abuse? She could represent so many women today. Her rebelling was a threat to the male dominance of the day. The king, shocked and with bruised ego, consulted with his 'wise men', whose counsel was based on occult practices.

Ring any bells? Isn't it just a picture of modern society? Occult involvement, lawlessness, godless philosophies, bad attitudes, political correctness, materialism, corruption, pride, arrogance, self-indulgence, self-gratification, terrorism. These were the times of Esther, and these are the times of today. Into all that she was to step and take up her sovereign position on behalf of the ethnic minority. You too? That is the scene of her calling. The pressures of the age weighing heavily upon her shoulders.

A HIDDEN SPIRITUAL FACTOR

Chapter 3:1 mentions the Agagite. The connection began 1000 years previously when Saul was told to slaughter King Agag, king of the Amalekites. This was an atheistic society, opposing the people of God and God decreed its destruction. King Saul refused to put Agag to death, resulting in God's judgement upon him and the eventual removal of his crown. Here you see clearly the far-reaching consequences of a previous generation's disobedience. The 'personal' vendetta between Haman and Mordecai was not so personal. There was an underlying spiritual principle. The eruption of a 1000-year old volcano of antagonism. This conflict represented the forces of good and evil. Our nations are threatened by the assault of materialism and secularism.

The church itself is under similar attack. The world is influencing the church when it should be the exact opposite scenario. *Rom 12:2* exhorts us not to allow the world to press us into its mould.

The language of a pagan society infiltrates our children, our schools, our churches, our media, our spiritual climate. These were the times in which Esther came to fulfil her role as deliverer of her people and these are the times in which we are called to fulfil ours. People out there haven't got a chance without the taking up of the challenge by godly men and women, but with the stepping up to the plate comes the opportunity for a great deliverance.

Whatever your kingdom is, it too comes with a challenge. The time is short. Throughout scripture, God has appointed times, divine appointments. In due time, He sent forth His Son, also on a mission to save His people from the ravages of a sinful world.

*Now is **your** divine appointment.*

The challenge is, do you risk your own welfare, comfort and reputation? Or do you trust the wisdom, counsel and timing of God to use you as a channel to bring about a great deliverance for those who cannot otherwise bring about their own?

See too 'Responsibility Of Privilege'

Get a Revelation!!

Mark 8: 27-29

In this day and age there are many liberal viewpoints as to whom Jesus is. Jesus becomes popular or unpopular by public whim or fashion. He is in and out of vogue by the same dictate. He is put into many a mould or religion of convenience. A Jesus to fit your conscience or philosophy. Free with your favourite breakfast cereal.

But hey – get a revelation!

He said, "Who do *you* say that I am? "Only one answer is correct. *Not* all roads lead to heaven. *Not* any god will do. Only *One* has the words of eternal life. There is only One through whom you can come to the Father.

Who is He?

His name is Jesus. The Christ. The Anointed one. The Messiah. The Son of the living God. The Way, the Truth and the Life.

At His very Name every knee shall bow and every tongue confess that Jesus Christ is Lord, to the glory of God the Father. No other Name. No other way.

Get a revelation – Jesus *is* King of Kings and Lord of Lords.

Who do *you* say that I am? One day my friend, Jesus will require you to answer that very question. Get a revelation – **now!**

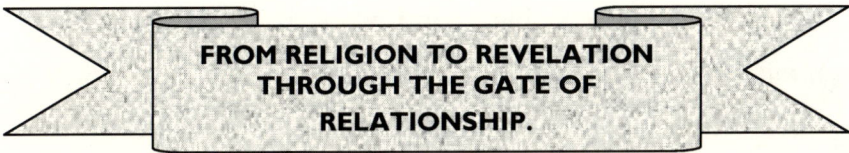

FROM RELIGION TO REVELATION THROUGH THE GATE OF RELATIONSHIP.

Check it out: Jn 14:6, Phil 2:10-11, 1 Tim 6:15

God-Given Gifts

Moses was called by God to lead the people of Israel out of Egypt but he protested, telling the Lord that he wasn't able or capable. God however, wanted a vessel through whom He could work to achieve His purposes for His nation. It wasn't what Moses could do; it was what God could do through him. God wasn't looking for capability, but availability. Not perfection, rather willingness.

He told Moses "*Now then go, and I, even I, will be with your mouth, and teach you what you are to say*" (*Ex 4:12*). If God puts His weight behind what He gives you, there's going to be a power explosion. Sometimes we don't even recognise that we have a potential enabling, but God sees it, and others will recognise it. The Lord was with Moses' mouth because that was where God had placed the anointing in his life. Whatever your gift or calling is, God will be with it and in it. He will cause you to discover your gift and step out in it. Whom He appoints, He anoints.

The bible says that "the *gifts and the calling of God are irrevocable*" (*Rom 11:29*). They are not taken away if we fail. They will develop as our character develops and as we apply ourselves to the gift.

50

We cannot take people further than we ourselves have gone and we need to remember that God-given gifts are not for our benefit. They are given to help others grow, mature and find their own place of service in the Body of Christ. We must therefore act responsibly concerning our gift, doing what is necessary to develop it to the very best standard of excellence. Go to relevant seminars and conferences. Get around those that are further on in the same gifting and ask questions. *You* are a gift to the Body.

My own journey of training in teaching the Word of God has included time in Ministers Class when as youth we were given assignments to complete, listening to other teachers, studying, reading, discussion, writing down of thoughts, ideas, phrases, lines from songs, being observant, practice, having wise mentors.

"He (Jesus) opened his mouth and began to teach them, saying..." (*Mat 5:2*). To teach, it is necessary to open your mouth! Quite obvious, but whatever your gift is you simply need to begin to do it! When Jesus opened His mouth and spoke, the people marvelled. Why! Because He spoke with authority and not as the legalistic leaders of the day. (*Mat 7:28-29*)

Scripture tells us that our gift will make room for us, so we need to create some space and use it! God will be in it and will direct your steps.

If your gift is teaching, begin by sitting down with a friend, open up the Word and share what God has given you. It probably won't mean you fill a stadium overnight, but start where you are.

Jesus was *"teaching many things in parables"* (Mk 4:2). Stories and illustrations from everyday life that people could relate to. Keep it simple and find some common ground for folks to understand. Many times when I am gardening, God will speak to me with the illustration of a flower – or a weed! For example, have you ever noticed that a weed often looks remarkably similar to the plant it is growing alongside! Take a look. There's a whole message there on the counterfeit works of the enemy, or the wheat and tares growing together.

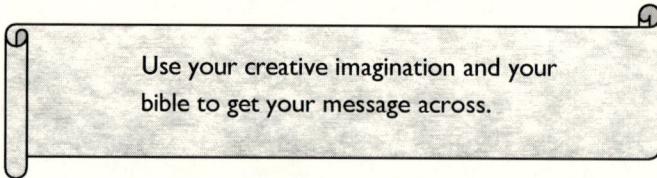

> Use your creative imagination and your bible to get your message across.

Pray about your gift. In the Psalms David often asked the Lord to teach him – to pray, to do His will, to follow His paths, to stay pure, and so on. Ask God to teach you about your gift.

Lk 12:12 – *"for the Holy Spirit will teach you."* Stay filled with the Spirit and He will give you thoughts, ideas, revelation.

Jn 7:16-18 – *"My teaching is not Mine, but His who sent Me. If anyone is willing to do His will, he will know of the teaching, whether it is of God or whether I speak from Myself. He who speaks from himself seeks his own glory; but He who is seeking the glory of the One who sent Him, He is true, and there is no unrighteousness in Him."* This is very important! What is the purpose of your gift and why do you want to use it! We must always check ourselves because it is easy to want the approval of man, or to want to impress.

God may not mind that in the beginning, but with any gift, it will carry impact and anointing to the degree that we use it as a representative of God and are yielded to Him in exercising it. The first call of the disciples was to *"Follow Him"*, to come out of the ordinary and step into the radical. First of all into a relationship. Any calling or gifting comes out of a deepening walk with Jesus.

Whereas we can learn much from others, their techniques and even their doctrine, remember that everyone is unique with their own temperament, character and personality. God is a God of variety and by the Holy Spirit He gives gifts *"just as He wills"* (*1 Cor 12:11*). Ten teachers will each present the same truth in a varied manner according to who they are, the path they have walked, personality, style, and even culture. That's the beauty of God. No fingerprint or snowflake is alike. Untold possibilities. Limitless. Boundless. No cloning with God. He loves variety.

Never compare yourself with someone else. He personally designed your uniqueness and individuality.

Make room for one another so that the gifts can be released, the Body can grow and be blessed, and the Kingdom of God can be multiplied to the nations, bringing glory to the King – that should always be our ultimate goal.

Check it out: I Cor 12:1, 4-11, 28-31, I Cor 14:1, 12

God Of Suddenly

I love the 'suddenlies' of God in the Bible. Those occasions when God shows up and takes your breath away. You're going about your normal business and *suddenly* – here comes heaven!

*"Shepherds ... keeping watch over their flock by night. And an angel of the Lord **suddenly** stood before them, ... and **suddenly** there appeared with the angel a multitude of the heavenly host praising God" (Lk2:9,13).* UFO's about? No, just an unexpected invasion by an angel and the butting in of a multitude of the heavenly host who could not contain themselves at the birth of a Saviour, Christ the Lord, into the world. The fulfilment of Prophecy.

Or take the disciples gathered together in the Upper Room on the Day of Pentecost. Unity brought a **suddenly** as heaven again broke in upon the scene as the Holy Spirit noisily and violently filled the house and those assembled *(Acts 2:2)*. The fulfilment of Promise *(Jn 16:7-14)*.

How about Saul of Tarsus? Merrily on his way to abuse, persecute and murder more believers, when **suddenly** a lightning bolt from heaven struck him down and put his lights out! Apprehended by the glorious Presence of God, the Final Authority *(Acts 9:3, 22:6)*. The fulfilment of Purpose.

Now a believer, Paul with Silas, were beaten and imprisoned for their faith. In their darkest hour they were *"praying and singing hymns of praise to God"* when **suddenly** *there came a great earthquake."* Heaven shaking the foundations of the prison house, breaking loose the chains from the captives and flinging wide the cell doors *(Acts 16:26)*. The fulfilment of Power.

Sovereign **'suddenlies'** fulfil prophecy and promise, reveal God's purpose and display His evident power.

Expect the God of **'Suddenly'** to send heaven into *your* situation!

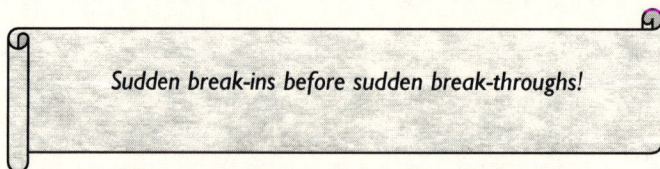

Sudden break-ins before sudden break-throughs!

See 'Suddenly' in WORDSONGS

Immediately

I call Mark's gospel the **'immediately'** gospel. The word hits me every-time I turn its pages.

With Jesus on the scene, there's always something happening, and initially I was left breathless at the pace of the Divine Action-Man! I think Mark must have marvelled a little himself from the way events are recorded. Jesus certainly caused a stir everywhere He went.

What this gospel demonstrates is the power and authority of Jesus and His no-nonsense approach to salvation. *"I came to set the captives free!" (Lk 4:18).*

Immediately

Check it out : Here are a few verses to start you off –

Mk 1:10, 18, 20, 21, 28, 29, 42, 2:8, 12, 5:29-30, 42, See also Mat 20 :34, Lk 3:13, Rev 4:2

In The Place of Worship

Have you ever had times when you have sensed such a reality of the presence of God that you didn't know what to do or say? Times when you could hardly believe, much less describe your experience?

That happened occasionally with the disciples. Although there were twelve of them, all of whom were being taught and trained by Jesus, it was very often the case that the 'inner circle' of three were privileged to be present on extraordinary occasions.

Peter, James and John held a divine place and purpose in Jesus' life. He knew their need for a greater revelation and understanding of God's purposes. He also knew that 'these three' would be pillars in the Church that was soon to be birthed. They were far from perfect and would fail many times, but the Father saw their potential, Jesus saw their hearts and He was imparting eternal truths during His short time with them on earth. He was opening up their understanding of Who he was, and building a foundation of faith upon which His Church would be built.

One such instance was when Jesus took the three up a high mountain, alone with Him. You see,

> *If you want to touch heaven you have*
> *to be prepared to leave earth behind*

You will need to get away from the crowds, even from friends, family, familiarity, anything that might distract – and escape for some 'alone' time with God. You will never be disappointed and you will grow spiritually in amazing ways.

The disciples could not have *begun* to imagine what was to take place next. We're told that Jesus was 'transfigured' before their eyes. They saw such a change taking place that His clothes became radiant and white with the glory of God 'as no launderer on earth can whiten them'. Wow! That's what happens when we bring our earth-soiled lives before Almighty God. Transformation occurs when we stand in the place of worship. His powerful Presence decontaminates us from all the world's sin and decay. We are washed not with launderer's soap but with the precious blood of the Lord Jesus and we are changed eternally. He puts the light back into our lives.

We're told that the angels come and go before the presence of God. Their appearance is awesome and often brings fear to the hearts of man. Very often the angels came to earth with a message from God and their first words spoken were "Fear not".

Powerful beings displaying the very glory of God such that it seemed as though lightning was emanating from them. How much more the glorious heavenly transfiguration of Jesus?

Transfiguration

You know, one day the same experience will be ours. We are travellers on this earth, not settlers. Our citizenship is in heaven ... and our body will be transformed ... into conformity with the body of His glory.

Hallelujah!

In other words, we will become like the Lord Jesus Christ in heavenly form. Our earthly trappings will be shed! That's true in the natural and in the spiritual. Changed from one degree of glory to another here in our walk with God and then the work that He has begun in us will be made complete.

One day we shall be like Him, we shall know Him as He knows us – completely.

This passage of scripture shows that as Jesus was being 'transfigured', Elijah and Moses appeared on the scene.

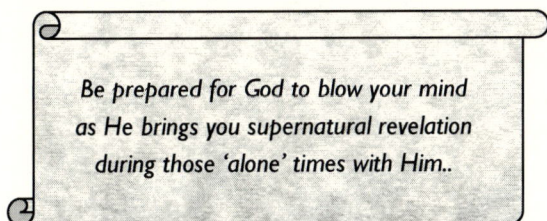

> Be prepared for God to blow your mind
> as He brings you supernatural revelation
> during those 'alone' times with Him..

World circumstances in these end times are such that you will need to be supernaturally equipped to deal with them. Make sure you are equipped ahead of time. God will, by the power of the Holy Spirit, give you wisdom and strategy

Elijah represented the prophets and Moses the Law. Jesus the Word made flesh came to fulfil both through His birth, death and resurrection. The disciples saw them talking with Jesus ...yet Peter answered! Check it out! He really was so overcome and terrified he did not know what to say or how to behave. Our 'human-ness' can appear very foolish when in the presence of Glory! Or we can so marvel at a move of God that we want to camp on it, as Peter did.

As if this wasn't enough for Peter and the others to get their heads around, a cloud, the Divine Presence of God, then descended and overshadowed them.

If he was trembling before, this must have frozen his flesh! The very voice of Almighty Father God boomed out over the mountain. It would have seemed like thunder or an earthquake. *"This is My beloved Son, with Whom I am well pleased. Listen to Him!"* Keep quiet Peter! Isn't that what Father God wants of us too? When we can't explain it all away – be still and know that He is God.

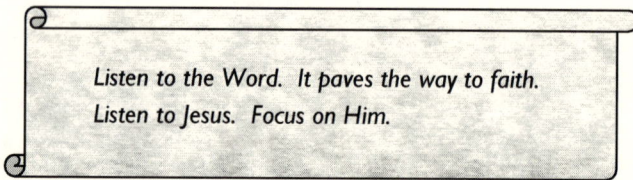

> *Listen to the Word. It paves the way to faith.*
> *Listen to Jesus. Focus on Him.*

Suddenly the spectacular was gone and the disciples were alone with Jesus. Heaven and earth will pass away – but the Word of God will remain forever. It's good to have times when we encounter the marvellous and miraculous. Wonderful and significant as those experiences are, they are not all we build our faith and Christian life upon.

Jesus Christ, the Word made flesh is our Rock, our Anchor, our Hope, our Salvation. When the world goes out, Jesus is still there. Ever present. Ever true. Ever faithful.

The disciples had to come down from the mountain. They'd spent precious time with their Lord. Eternity had been invested in their hearts.

They had many questions, much to tell but they were instructed to say nothing until Jesus was raised from the dead. Hard for the Peters of this world!

Intimate moments aren't always meant to be shared. Savour them. Ponder them. Cherish them. Allow God to lead you along the path of wisdom and teach you what to say and when to say it. Timing is important. The One who is The Way, The Truth and The life will show you.

Check it out: Ps 24:3, Mat 28:2-4, Phil 3:20-21, 1 Cor 13:12, Ps 46:10, Mk 13:31, Heb 13:8

Jesus Who?

Jesus was conceived of the Holy Spirit (*Lk 1:31, 35, Mat 1:20*) and born of a young virgin girl (*Is 7:14*) who was told that He would be called the Son of God (*Lk 1:32*) and that His name Jesus meant One Who saves His people from their sins (*Mat 1:21*). Local shepherds were told that He was the Saviour, Christ the Lord (*Lk 2:11*). Wise men, astrologers, sought him out (*Mat 2:1-2*).

The blood of an infant comes from the father. God the Father's blood ran through Jesus. Holy blood that would eventually be shed and presented back to the Father and accepted by Him as the perfect, once-for-all sacrifice to cover our sins and bring us back into relationship with Him. Although Joseph was the earthly step-father, he had no involvement in the bringing of Jesus into the world (*Mat 1:25*).

Jesus was born in Bethlehem (*Lk 2:4-7*) but lived and was raised in Nazareth, a city in Galilee (*Lk 2:39*). He grew and became strong, increasing in wisdom in His relationship with God and man, and grace (joy, favour, acceptance, kindness, loving-kindness) (*Lk 2:40, 51-52*), and knew right from wrong at the age of eating curds and honey (Is 7:15).

This tells us that He was teachable, obedient and submissive to His parents, developing both physical stature and spiritual character (Lk 2:51-2).

When He became 12 He accompanied His parents to Jerusalem for the Feast of the Passover. His earthly parents did not fully understand the calling on Jesus' life and were shocked to find that He did not return with them but was to be found in the Temple both listening to the teachers and asking profound questions of them, amazing His hearers with His understanding of the Word. (Lk 2:41-50). He was discovering from scriptures and prophecy that He was the Word made flesh and was to be the Passover Lamb and had an increasing hunger to fulfil that calling.

He went about everyday life for many years, learning carpentry skills, being taught the scriptures, and forming relationships. Living in the natural. The spiritual would follow.

At the approximate age of thirty years, Jesus came to the Jordan river to be baptised of John the Baptist, identifying with humanity as the Son of Man and submitting Himself to His Father in prayer.

It was at that moment that the heavens were opened and a spiritual baptism also took place as the Holy Spirit visibly clothed Him in readiness for ministry and He received the recognition of spiritual Sonship by His heavenly Father, appointed as His power of attorney for the good works of the gospel (*Lk 3:21-22*).

He was led from there into the wilderness where for forty days he was tempted by the devil with all that might lure Him from His mission. Jesus countered every attack with the Word of God, gaining strength, until the devil departed from Him (*Lk 4:1-13*). Jesus went *into* the desert full of the anointing of the Holy Spirit, but He came through the testing and out *from* the desert in the *power* of that anointing, equipped to begin His earthly ministry (*Lk 4:14-15*). He knew from prophecy what He had been sent to do (*Lk 4:18-19, 21*). His was a ministry with signs and wonders following that would see people saved, healed, delivered, set free and given life, seeing their eternal relationship with God the Father restored.

He was the Word made flesh (*Jn 1:1*) and He took upon Himself the form of a servant, becoming obedient to fulfil His Fathers' commission to take upon Himself the sin of the world upon a cross. For this reason God has honoured Him (*Phil 2:5-11*). He knew Who He was and what His rights were, but He chose not to exercise them. He laid down His life for the many. He always had the interest of others at heart.

66

He was a people person. He came to meet needs. To show unconditional love. To set captives free (*Lk 4:18*). To be the one mediator between God and man (*Heb 12:24*). To provide forgiveness of sin (*Mat 26:28*). To give eternal life (*Jn 17:2*). To reconcile man to God (*Eph 2:16*). He cut straight through traditions and binding laws and gave recognition to the poor, lowly and outcast, radically honouring, recognising and including women and society's cast-offs among His number.

He knew Who He was, where He had come from, where He was going, so had vision, purpose and security enough to show how to serve others rather than be served (*Jn 13:3-5*).

He is the Author and Finisher of our faith and had great joy in enduring the agony of suffering, despising the shame, and able to call out to His Father from the cross, *"It is finished!"* (Jn 19:30), 'I've completed the work You gave me to do. I'm coming home!'

Jesus is our great example. Let's follow Him all the way to glory!

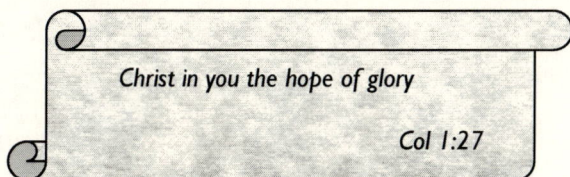

Christ in you the hope of glory

Col 1:27

Lighten Up

Gen 1:1 *"In the beginning God created the heavens and the earth."* This is a statement of fact. The Holy Spirit doesn't waste words. No small talk. No speculation. No opinion. No justification or need for explanation.

Is 45:18 *"For the Lord is God and He created the heavens and the earth and put everything in place, He made the world to be lived in, not to be a place of empty chaos."* (NLT) Statement of fact. Our God *is*.

Psalms tells us that *"the earth is the LORD'S and all it contains"* (Ps 24:1). Everything belongs to Him. He owns the cattle on a thousand hills. (Ps 50:10). Another statement of fact.

There is always a beginning with God, the One Who is called Alpha, and there will therefore always be a hope and a future. He loves to break in on a scene of complete darkness, and begin to restore life and order. God's excited by a challenge. He simply applies the opposite force and proclaims *"Let there be light!"* God reveals Himself through His works, which unfold His very nature.

Miracles are the realm in which God operates and in which He specialises.

Jn 1:1-5 "In the beginning the Word already existed. He was with God, and He was God. He was in the beginning with God. He created everything there is. Nothing exists that He didn't make. Life itself was in Him, and this light gives life to everyone. The light shines through the darkness, and the darkness can never extinguish it." (NLT)

Lk 1:78-9 "Because of God's tender mercy, the light from heaven is about to break upon us, to give light to those who sit in darkness and in the shadow of death, and to guide us to the path of peace." (NLT)

Rom 8:28 "God causes everything to work together for the good of those who love God and are called according to His purpose for them." (NLT)

These verses show us a God Who is well able to break into circumstances that seem dark and hopeless, Who takes up the challenge of change and brings good out of them.

Gen 1:2 "The earth was empty, a formless mass cloaked in darkness. And the Spirit of God was hovering over its surface." (NLT) Something 'happened' somewhere in time, causing potential disaster.

This was a seemingly grim and hopeless situation in which only God could intervene. Many can identify with and apply this to life's experiences. Formless and void describes emptiness, but God's Word is key here. He and His Word are one. In the same manner as God, we must take Him at His Word and apply it to those circumstances in sword-like thrusts that pierce the darkness and let in His light. The Word is sharp, powerful and alive to cut right hrough the formless mass and allow the Spirit of God to intervene and establish order.

Gen 1:1 sees God as Creator and *Gen 1:2* sees Him as Redeemer/Restorer, intervening to bring light and life into a dead scenario. This is the gospel.

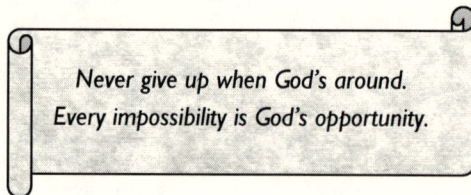

> *Never give up when God's around.*
> *Every impossibility is God's opportunity.*

The power of the Holy Spirit is always there and available. He hovered over the scene, anticipating the Word of God that would release His creative/restorative energy.

Order was about to be established! Things were going to take shape, no doubt bringing colossal change. That is often the case when God shows up.

Gen 1:3 When God decrees a thing, it becomes done. Something of God Himself was deposited in Creation as His energy was released. Read *Colossians 1:13-18* to see how our spiritual rebirth mirrors the work of creation. Into natural and worldly darkness God brings His spiritual Light – the Incomparable Christ.

Reflection or meditation on the contrasts in our lives can be helpful to appreciate and understand the opposites. If no darkness, there could be no appreciation of light, if no sorrow, no delight in joy, if no death, no gratitude for life. When weak, we are encouraged by the return of strength.

God did not dispense with the darkness. He used it. We need to do the same and allow the Holy Spirit to overshadow us, touch us, work with us so that we begin to see God's perspective. He sees potential in everything and uses it for His good and glory. He makes a way where there seems to be no way. He applied the opposite force to the darkness and actually used it to establish His creative order! He simply spoke into the darkness. Hallo? So simple, yet so profound. Speak God's truth into dark situations.

It will be as though the light has been turned on. It will start to separate good from the bad, the wood from the trees, the light from the dark.

Both the light and the dark were under God's control and each had a function. All that God does is with a view to bringing blessing to life. He spoke ten creative commandments, each establishing an environment into which He could ultimately place His crowning glory - man.

He also separated water from water. There was too much on the earth and some of it was removed and stored in the sky or firmament (the heavens) when it was created. The account of Noah tells of the floodgates of heaven being closed to allow the Flood to subside.

> *Perhaps it is that at times God causes separation, dividing, removing, a drawing away because He has other plans and purposes.*

A separation from worldliness. These verses show us a God Who is well able to break into situations that seem dark and hopeless, Who takes up the challenge of change and brings good out of them. We never see God discarding, but redistributing. The water above the firmament was ultimately used by way of judgement, to cleanse the earth and remove sin.

When God created the myriad of stars, scripture tells us that He called them each by name and set them all in place. He appointed them to function alongside the great light, and to govern the night and day. Isn't our purpose to do exactly that too? We have been chosen by name, set where we are and appointed to function as lights alongside, and in constant co-operation with, the Light of the World. God's church should be a corporate light in the world and the challenge to us is to walk in the light as He is in the light.

The story of Creation is a pattern of new life and new birth in Christ. *Genesis* is a blueprint for the ways, character and workings of God throughout scripture. Right in the beginning His righteousness, holiness, godliness and goodness are revealed as He spoke into the darkness, "Light – BE!"

Creation

Check It Out : Eph 6:12, I Jn 1:5-7, Eph 4:17-18

Loud, Brash and ... 'Out There!'

PS 117 – A Psalm of Praise

Two verses – packed with meaning! A little appetiser of teaching.

This is called a "Psalm or Song of Praise" and V2 will give us some reasons why we should live from 'an attitude of gratitude'.

V1 – "praise the Lord all nations". I'd say that includes everyone, wouldn't you? Even you and I? In Hebrew, the word 'praise' here is 'halal'. A mini Hebrew lesson too! Now, 'halal' is obviously associated with sound, would you agree? 'Praise Him on the *loud* cymbals' etc. It's pretty obvious that praise is not a silent thing – c/f heaven! Neither is praise a passive thing. 'I praise God in my own way – inwardly'. No, God's way is loud and brash and 'out there'. It's very active!

So we know already two things about 'halal' – loud and active. I expect you'll say 'we know all that', but the challenge is, are we doing the part of God's Word that we *do* know?

We all love 'fresh revelation' and sometimes we feel empty or dry yet if we actually take just one verse like this and activate it in our lives, then we find we're starting to get filled again.

Did you know that laughter, real deep belly laughing is so extremely good for our health, and for our souls? It's so freeing too. There should be over**flow** in/from our lives, not occasional 'drips of experience'. OK – so praise carries with it sound and action.

Did you also know that there is also another aspect to the root meaning of 'halal'? Ready? Sound, action, and … colour! Catch this! It doesn't mean putting on your brightest clothes or waving luminous flags about, although of course you may! It is a word rich in meaning. It means 'to shine, to make a show, to boast, to be completely uninhibited', even foolish in the sense of throwing off all restraint. It has the sense of 'being light'. To be free enough to celebrate and give God all the glory. Does it remind you of anyone? Remember David dancing before the Lord as the Ark of the Covenant was restored to Jerusalem? Some, including his wife, thought he was mad. *(2 Sam 6:14-16)*. So joy-filled was he that he had thrown off *every* restraint and inhibition! He didn't care what anyone else thought. That's what God is looking for – those that will worship Him in Spirit and in truth – not considering the flesh, but acting according to what is right in God's Word.

Even those closest to you may not understand or agree, but who are we serving, God or man?

David was utterly overjoyed that the Presence of the Lord was being restored to Israel – the protection, blessing and Covenant relationship and all that it represented. Do we get that overjoyed over our salvation and the continual presence of God in our lives?

At the heart of 'halal' is the meaning of sheer radiance. We all know the word 'hallelujah'. It's the same word all over the world. It's a form of rejoicing and giving of glory to God. We sing 'Shine Jesus Shine'. Jesus shone! He *was* the radiance of God. The Light of the World and we are called to be as He is in the world. When we're dull or down there's a darkness about us. Light attracts, and that's what we are called to be – *attractive*!

So, that's the first word in this psalm! ***"Praise the Lord!"*** It's a command, not a suggestion. Why? Because it will carry you through the storms of life and give you strength.

Still *VI – "Praise the Lord all **nations**."* It's a very general word and covers all peoples, tribes, nations and particularly the non-Jewish or pagan nations. Wow! Now catch this – here's the heart of God if you need a reason to rejoice. Why is it important that all the nations learn to 'halal' or exuberantly praise God?

76

Here it is – because God planned to save them through the Messiah! He saw it. He knew it way in advance of us finding out! Awesome.

"Laud Him" – God's getting excited here. Do you know that when someone is excited their voice gets louder and louder and you can't ignore it? That's what is happening here. Laud – is loud! To be loud. To praise God for His mighty acts.

Now 'laud' can also be used to pacify or calm anger through words and to still waves. To soothe with praises.

Ps 65:7 –to still the raging seas. It's the same word. Are you getting the picture? Reminds us of Jesus speaking to the storm and commanding the waves to be still. I don't think Jesus would have been whispering to the great waters do you? I believe He spoke order into chaos. Did you know that your loud praises will still the voice and works of the enemy in your life?

> *Your exuberant joy and loud gladness will cause the enemy to flee and you will take the sting out of his tail as you bring triumphant praise into your situations.*

Jesus didn't argue with the storm. He spoke out of Who He was and the wind and the waves obeyed. Jesus knew He had come from the Father and was returning to Him.

Everything else in between was almost a pause in time. He came with God's authority to complete the assignment given to Him. Why should it be any different for us?

*"Laud Him all **peoples**."* All peoples means – all peoples! No exceptions.

So *V1* – be loud, be active, be joyful, shine, be uninhibited, be excited, be attractive and share God's enthusiasm for life, with the authority that is yours in Christ.

That's the 'what' and V2 gives us the 'why'. Are you ready for V2?

V2 – *"For His loving-kindness is great towards us."* "Checed" (Hesed), or loving-kindness is one of the most important words in the bible. Love is a covenant word and God is love. It's closely related to the forgiveness of sins. God's loving-kindness is eternal. It's an attitude of love which contains mercy. Faithfulness, loyalty, beauty, unfailing love, favour – all these are connected with the merciful love of God. Our response should be to return to Him our total gratitude and praise.

love one another

"*And the truth of the Lord is everlasting*". The firmness, stability, sureness, faithfulness – this is the truth of God and about God.

Doesn't it remind you of the **Rock**? A sure foundation. Immovable. Unshakeable. Shouldn't all this draw an automatic response of thankful praise and adoration to our God?

"*Everlasting*" – from time immemorial into eternity, the distant past into unending future that we cannot begin to comprehend. Perpetual. Without end. Never a second when His solid Presence wasn't there. That's why one of His Names is 'Shammah' – the God who is 'there'. The Psalmist states that there is nowhere we can hide from God's love and presence. Not a moment in time when His unfailing merciful love isn't reaching out to us. So close He hears our thoughts, He counts the hairs on our head, He wipes every tear. So close. So near. So beautiful.

What is there more to say than *'Praise the Lord'*. The Lord Jehovah. The Lord Emmanuel. The Lord Almighty. The Lord mighty to save. The God who heals. The Lord our Banner. The Lord our Provider. The Lord the Lifter of our Heads. What you need Him to be, He is.

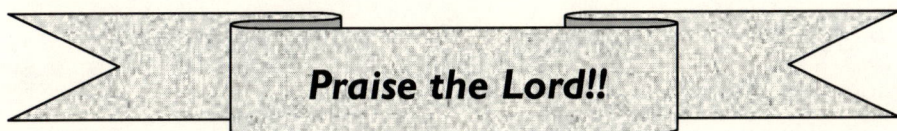

Praise the Lord!!

Responsibility of Privilege

Esther 4:14

"If you remain silent this time ... who knows but that you have come to the kingdom for such a time as this."

Mat 11:12 "the kingdom of heaven suffers violence, and violent men take it by force."

Perhaps you feel you have no real identity and are of no significance, with no important voice. Yet as believers God tells us that we are strategically crucial to His purposes and often the very means He uses to bring them about. We aren't here at all for our own ends. We're citizens of heaven, ambassadors representing the Kingdom of God.

You may question what one person can achieve. Moses, Abraham, Gideon and many others felt the same. On your own you can't make a difference, but your mattering and your achieving is all in Christ! Through Him you can do exploits! You can accomplish those things because He strengthens or anoints you to do so. When you are weak He can display His strength through you.

80

Wherever you are, in that home, family, college, house-group, church, business, hospital, even prison, you can be there as a living testimony of God's grace. God's Word says that God's people perish without a vision. See yourself and your purpose in Him. You're here to challenge the culture, not to go with it. To be salt and light. Where there's injustice, make a stand. Write a letter. Make a 'phone call. Stand against unlawfulness. Prayer was removed from our schools many years ago because a strong individual made a stand, and Christians did nothing to prevent it. Don't compromise.

Be a light shining in a dark place.

If you don't fulfil your calling, God will find another channel because He is sovereign, but what a sad day it will be when we have to explain away our reluctance, fear or apathy. Don't be passed over by the Holy Spirit as He seeks to administer a plan in which He purposed you would play a vital role. Develop a friendship with the Holy Spirit. Spend time in prayer and in the Word and let Him teach and train your ear. He'll give you a plan, and always the strategy with which to execute it.

There are consequences in remaining silent. Remaining silent is a picture of prayerlessness. If we don't take up our position of prayer (and fasting when necessary) and call out to God in intercession for our homes, families, businesses, towns, cities, nations, then we will all suffer the consequences of that negligence.

We won't escape. How much is the church responsible for and suffering the results of its failure to speak out on moral issues? The world is also suffering the outcome of our silence. It conveys weakness in the eyes of a world that is looking for and expecting the church to do and be something of which it declares it stands for – truth and righteousness.

If someone has an abundance of food and another is hungry, it would be criminal not to share that plenty with those who are starving. In Christ we have an abundance. Rivers of Living Water. The Bread of Life. Grace upon grace.

If we maintain silence for any reason, usually because it's far more comfortable to do so, then we stand guilty before the Lord. He says that by our words we shall be justified and by our words we shall be condemned. Could it be that our lack of words carries the same implication? Sins of commission and also sins of omission. Jesus said *"I must work the works of God."* Paul *said "Woe is me if I don't preach the gospel to this broken world."* That should be our heartbeat.

> *Impelled to speak and act – for such a time as this.*

Check it out : Mat 12:36-7, Jn 9:4, 1 Cor 9:16

See too 'For Such A Time As This'

Stand And Deliver

You stand and God *will* deliver!

Jehoshophat

Jehoshophat became king of Judah, reigning for 25 years. He was a good king and the Lord was with him *(2 Ch 17)* such that he became great, with much riches and honour. The kingdom was made strong under his rule. He established judges for fair rule and turned the people of Israel back to the Lord, always exhorting them to fear God and live righteously. It was a time of restoration and God's favour for Israel, a parallel with what God is currently doing among His people.

2 Chron Ch 20

V1 Israel was experiencing severe harassment from her enemies. Sound familiar? They had come to pick a fight, to make war. A sense of darkness and foreboding loomed.

V2-3a When he heard the news, Jehoshophat was *alarmed* at the prospect of invasion. When things are actually spoken out to us, they very often have a profound effect.

Terror, fear and panic are often the first fiery darts the enemy hurls at us and they come at us with full force - don't they, especially if we're committed to God's purposes. God deals with truth, with realities. Jehoshophat was real. It doesn't say he covered himself with the blood, confessed all the victory scriptures he could remember and then scoffed at the enemy. It says he was alarmed! That's real! That's our humanity. If the devil can get us discouraged, he's got us defeated.

V3b This man knew where to go for help. Most of us go to the 'phone first, but Jehoshophat went to the Throne and sought the Lord. David often did that. He was always in all sorts of terrifying situations, but he knew his God, and enquired of Him. That's the first thing we need to get into the habit of when we're in trouble. **Seek the Lord**.

V4 *Then*, he **shared** his dilemma **with others**. It's *good* to have those around you who can give you wise and godly counsel. Make sure you go to the *right* people. Be in relationship with the godly-wise, not the worldly-wise. There's also power in the corporate prayer anointing. He sought to unite the people in **prayer and intercession**.

Isn't that what we need to do more and more? We *need* the Body of Christ. You know, the days of the lone ranger are well and truly *over*. Many Christians say "I've been let down so much in the past, that I can't afford to share my problems with others any more". I tell you, you can't afford *not* to! These are the last days and we're going to need to stand together more and more and more, and know the support, the strength, the power of being united in prayer in one Body and with one accord.

Jehoshophat knew that. He knew the enemy wasn't among his own people. It was outside foes. It's time to do away with all differences among ourselves, and to come together as living stones, being built together by God into a beautiful Bride, and into a mighty army.

So, **"Seek the Lord, Come together** in **Prayer and Intercession."** *Ps 133* is a wonderful picture of the blessings of unity.

Next, Jehoshophat proclaimed a **Fast**. Oh dear. Self-denial and sacrifice. Drastic circumstances, drastic measures called for. *Is 58: 6-14, Joel 2: 12-13. You* ponder those scriptures and allow God to speak to you. Rend your heart. Get it right before God.

> *Prepare a way of holiness in your life.*

Get rid of all sin and hypocrisy, wilfulness and disobedience. *Then* the restoring can take place. *Then* the anointing will come. We've got to do it God's way if we want success.

V5-12 **Stand up!** *Eph 6:13-14 - Stand!!* Jehoshophat needed to be *seen* and *heard*. He declared the facts in prayer to God. He poured out his heart to the Lord. This is my dilemma, God. *Do* that. Stand up on the inside and lay out your problems before Him. (The believers in *Acts 4* did exactly the same just after Peter and John had been released from prison and the church was under attack). It's also a declaration to the enemy, that you're coming from the *stand*point of speaking out who God is in the situation. Not just having a pity party, but "these are the facts Lord, and this is who *You* are. Now arise and be God in this situation". It also builds *your* faith as you hear your positive confession of truth. Jehoshophat couldn't change anything. You can't either in your own strength, but you know a God who can! *V9* We *will* stand.

V6 **Speak up!** Confess God's word. Declare who He is.

RAISE UP A BANNER OF ALLEGIANCE TO THE KING!

We've got to be those who can be trusted with God's power, and can use it correctly.

We've got to be those who are crumple-proof! Trees that are planted by streams of water, and who don't dry out or crack up, but who produce fruit in season and out. To do that, we've got to know who we are in Christ, but most important, we've got to know who our God is.

V12 I Cor 2. Seek God's hidden wisdom. He's not hidden any truth *from* you, He's hidden it *for* you. Seek, and you shall find. As Paul says in the epistles, don't come with your own intelligence or eloquence. Know nothing except Christ crucified. Come in weakness (humility), fear and trembling, but with the Spirit's power. He'll teach you spiritual truths.

Ps 112 : 1,7 "Blessed is the man who fears the Lord, who greatly delights in His commandments. He will not fear evil tidings; his heart is steadfast, trusting in the Lord". Fix your eyes, fix your heart, fix your hope. Call upon the Lord. Soak yourself in Him.

2 Chron 7:14 " if my people, who are called by **my Name,** *humble themselves and pray,* **then** *I will hear from heaven, will forgive their sin and willl heal their land".*

V13 All stood. Everyone has got a place, a gift and a purpose in God's Body. No age limit. No sex discrimination with God. He's for whole families coming together to seek Him. Whole households for God.

Everyone is needed and everyone is required. There's no absenteeism once you've joined up in God's army. No deserters. Relationship is God's heart. It says *'all'*. No exceptions.

V14 "Then the Spirit of the Lord came" upon the prophet. As you pray and prophecy, so will come the anointing and the battle strategy. It may seem strange but so was Jericho. God's ways are not ours. We just need to follow! God won't keep you in the dark. How can He when He's the Light! He's laid a wonderful foundation for us through his prophets and apostles, and he continues to speak to us through **prophetic revelation**. Honour and use the gifts that God equips you with. They're vital to the building up of the Body and for the equipping of the saints ... not for bless me parties, but for works of service. Take the time to seek Him for a "now" word and expect to receive it! More than ever before, God is pouring out fresh revelation.

EXAMPLE OF BATTLE PLAN

Ex 14 : 13-14 "But Moses said the people, 'Do not fear. **Stand by** *and see the salvation of the Lord which He will accomplish for you today. The Lord will fight for you while you keep silent.'"* Don't fret or strive. Don't speak words which will negate God's. Be still ... and know that He is God.

V15   Seek, then **Listen.**

Lk 9:35   *"A voice came out of the cloud, saying 'This is my Son, My chosen One; listen to Him'"*

> *Listen to God. That's step one of success.*

Don't use your own wisdom.   Get God's thoughts and encouragement on the matter. James gives us a lot of guidance on which is better, earthly or spiritual wisdom. Take God's advice, He's got a bigger brain! Sometimes we can't find direction for our specific situation in God's word. He also says in *Rom 8* that He has given us His Spirit as a witness *inside* of us. We need to cultivate ears that hear the inner voice giving guidance and assurance.

Are you finding things getting tougher, blacker, more difficult? This is what the Lord says to you...."*Don't be afraid or discouraged because of this vast army*". God delights in a challenge!

V16 **Spiritual Warfare.**   *No* weapon formed against you shall prosper. That's God's counsel. The word 'formed' means something that is especially made with the express purpose of attacking you violently and rendering you defeated. What does God say ?

Forget it enemy. It won't work! The enemy has already been disarmed and made a spectacle of.

Move out. Let the enemy know you mean business. *You* know the battle is won, the enemy doesn't. Remind him. Remind him of his future.

V17 **Take up your position.** Not somebody else's. Find your place and get into it. Don't rush ahead of God, and don't do more than He requires of you. Move into position and **stand firm.** We don't have to fight the battles, we have to keep possession of what is already ours. How do we do that? What is our position? The next verse shows us.

Rom 5:1-2   By faith we stand.

Eph 6:13   We stand in what He has already done for us
      We stand complete in Him. Stand... and you *will* see the victory.

Josh 1:6   Be strong and courageous

Heb 10:25   Encourage one another

Eph 5:19   When you come together, speak out with psalms and hymns and spiritual songs. Edifying words!

God says, go and face your enemy. That's all. Shine your light into the face of the enemy. It's blinding!

Soldiers used to oil their shields and polish them like mirrors and when the sun shone on them as the enemy advanced, the light would dazzle and blind them and stop them in their tracks. They couldn't see a thing! That's it with us. Don't show the enemy your back. Shine your light full blast into his face. He can't stand it and he'll have to flee! The more oiled you are with God's anointing upon you, the greater a dazzler for God you'll become!

V18 How did Jehoshophat respond to God's word? What was the position God required him to take up? He got on the floor before God. He bowed down low and everyone followed. He led his people into **Worship**. See the progression. This is God's recipe for success. Get these ingredients in right measure and you're there! Always acknowledge the fact that it's God's power and grace that through our faith will deliver us. Know your God. Reverence Him.

V19 Priests and kings praising God together.

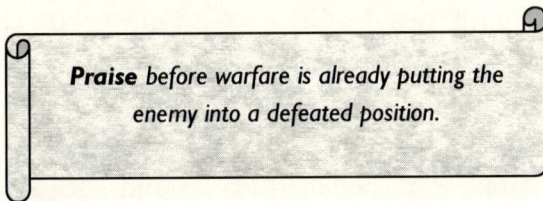

> **Praise** *before warfare is already putting the enemy into a defeated position.*

He hates it! The louder the better! David knew that too! He set the singers and musicians before the army didn't he? Weird strategy? No, it's just God's way to victory.

Don't mumble and grumble, stay humble. Watch your confession.

> *Praise and worship will break the strongholds of the enemy and you can then tear them down from a position of faith.*

V20 **Listen**. Keep listening. It's an ongoing process. Seek God's Word and counsel *all* the time. Your success is guaranteed. He says so! Early in the morning (before the heat and oppression of the day) they left for the desert. Get into position with God at a time of day when you're fresh and before the day's pressures come upon you.

Still a good leader, Jehoshophat keeps encouraging the people of Judah and Jerusalem to trust in God and His Word, maintaining their trust and focus.

When you're under pressure, don't back off, don't run away - **worship, praise and pray!** Go to **God's Word, stand firm, listen, praise** - loudly, and let faith be released.

V21 Good communication between leader and people. Important for success.

V22-3 What a mighty, faithful God we serve. We step out in faith and trust (trust and obey, for there's no other way to be happy in Jesus, but to trust and obey). Co-operate with Him. Look what happened - Israel sang, Israel praised - and the Lord sowed confusion and reaped havoc amongst Israel's foes. Simple isn't it when we get God's formula. The enemy very kindly finished the job by destroying each other. Remember Gideon? Same thing.

V24 The men of Judah (praise!) came and looked, and saw only dead bodies! A defeated foe. God never missed a single target - not one remained alive. His final outcome for the enemy.

V25 God blessed Israel's socks off! With the enemy's plunder. He says the wealth of the nations shall be given to us. We can **prosper** under His covenant promises. Don't just wish for pint-sized blessings and hope you can make it through today. No - that's *not* our God, unless you choose to place those restrictions upon Him. Look- it took three days to collect all the goodies! How great is *your* God? *That* big?

Are *you* willing to step out in faith? As you do, the power of God will be released more than you ever dreamed or imagined. You'll know His literal provision in many mighty ways, because it's part of God's covenant blessing. You'll see His power flowing and people in the world coming to be touched by God - through *you!*

V26 - 28 They're praising God again. Better get used to doing that folks. There they all are, gathered in the Valley of Beracah to praise the Lord. Beracah means praise. The people of praise praising in a place of praise. Make sure you keep coming to the place where you can fellowship and praise God together. They got themselves into a place where praise could be released and poured out. Have we?

There's a place of praise in every valley.

Applaud him. Extol him. Give Him *all* the glory. He's so worthy of it. Acknowledge that it's God's strategy, power, wisdom and faithfulness that delivers the enemy into your hands , but remember - you do what God instructs *you*, and you'll be richly blessed, encouraged, used and rewarded. They returned in triumph. So will you.

V29 And finally (my brethren), *"the fear of God came upon all the kingdoms and nations"*. That's the beginning of wisdom. The nations will learn godliness through God's people moving out and flowing with God in these days. There's a whole world looking, watching and waiting. Make sure they see God's saving power in your lives.

The floodgates in us will open up! *Not* power falling out of the sky, but God's word says - *"Out of your bellies shall flow streams of living water"*. The pure power of God will flow *from* us! It's from the inside out, that God is working.

Together, as God's army and God's Body, people will be washed into His Kingdom. Make sure you're not fighting each other! That's the *wrong* enemy.

V30 "The kingdom of Jehoshophat knew peace and rest on every side." That's part of God's blessing for us. Peace that passes all understanding with wholeness and prosperity in every area of life and victory in Jesus. You won't find it anywhere else. What a mighty God we serve!

This is a favourite passage of scripture, given to me of God during the trials and tribulations of a house purchase. When it seemed impossible, God turned it all around and made a way where there seemed to be none . My test of faith was to stand and worship, albeit at times through the tears.

Substance

When a potter considers his clay, when a sculptor contemplates his slab of marble, he waits until an image of the material's potential is formed on the inside of him before ever attempting to shape his masterpiece. He 'sees' the form of the completed work before beginning to craft or mould the un-fashioned shape.

He knows the capability and the pliability of the material. He is acutely aware of the ingredients of that particular substance; its strengths and weaknesses, how to handle it, how and where to apply the skills necessary to bring forth a finished work that will be a credit to its creator and reveal the beauty of the created. Shape, colour, form, personality, character. The completed work will contain all that is unique to it, yet also identifiable as belonging to the Creator. Injected into the work will be the DNA of the originator, somewhere the obvious signature of His matchless flair.

The verses here tell us that faith is the agency, the means, the confidence or assurance that what is not yet revealed externally has already been achieved and accomplished so far as God is concerned. Faith is God's building material. The Amplified Bible says that faith is the title deed of the things we hope for.   In other words, you can take it to the bank that the job is done in God's realm which operates through the medium of faith.

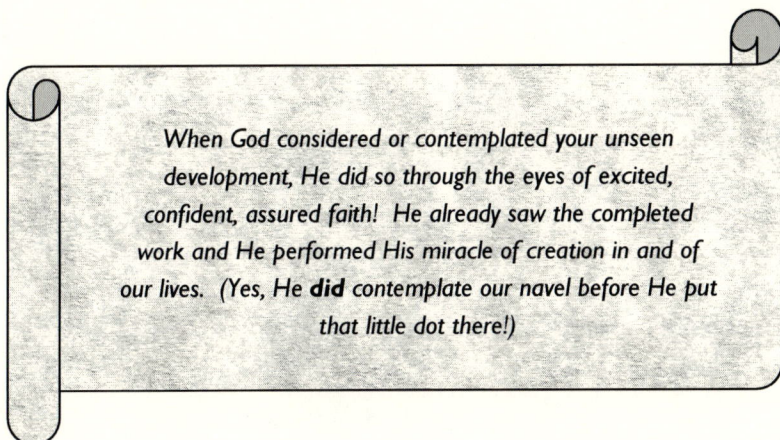

> *When God considered or contemplated your unseen development, He did so through the eyes of excited, confident, assured faith! He already saw the completed work and He performed His miracle of creation in and of our lives. (Yes, He **did** contemplate our navel before He put that little dot there!)*

In the same way as He created the heavens and the earth, He the Word, brought us forth into life and He says that He will go right on completing the development of our godly character until Christ be formed and the light of His glory (His DNA signature) be revealed in us.

At the end of the day we get to look just like our Heavenly Father!

Check it out :

> *Ps 139 : 16a "Your eyes saw my unformed substance"(Amp)*
> *Heb 11 : 1 "Now faith is the assurance (or substance) of things hoped for, the conviction (or evidence) of things not seen"*

Well Well Well

Wells had been dug by Abraham in a land promised to him and his descendants by God. He also had a 'lawful' right to dig them through an agreement made between him and Abimelech, who granted him permission to live in the land. Abraham – Isaac – Jacob – God's ongoing covenant promise from generation to generation, still in place.

We're told that the Philistines had stopped up all the wells with earth. The enemy's ploy will always be to try to hinder or impede the flow of God's blessings. The 'earth' here was envy and contention. The wells were stopped even though they were a valuable life source for everyone, including those blocking them! God's blessings are for all but some will deliberately try to prevent others from experiencing them, not realising that they themselves are losing out.

Isaac re-dug these old wells and other new ones. Perseverance and diligence were required. He had to dig deep to find a flow of water, and then check it back to its source. This was to remove blockages and to check for purity.

Allow God to dig deep and do the same work through His Word and His Holy Spirit in you, removing any sin pollution. The result will be that *"out of your innermost being shall flow rivers of living water"*. Whatever is put in is what will come out. Don't forget that wells are to supply others with life.

Isaac didn't find it easy. He was a stranger in the land and the enemy was at work seeking to rob, kill and destroy. As he opened up the old wells that had been dug by his father, he gave them the same names. He was honouring his father's memory and the Name of God. The wells would have been like memorial stones, representing perhaps an encounter with God, a promise received, a revelation given – unchangeable from generation to generation. Isaac was building on the work already started by God with his father Abraham. It required wisdom.

> *There is a time and place to dig into the past and a time and place not to.*

We can learn and benefit from past foundations laid, but we must also build on them and move forward. We have to work out our own salvation with God. We must learn to move with Him and not rely simply on what once worked if God has finished with it.

Wells can be found in the wilderness and in the valley. There is no situation where we cannot find God's promise, but we may have to dig deep to tap into it. There will be many wells of salvation in your desert. God supplies but we have to do our part. Isaac re-opened wells to re-introduce life to the land. For him, they were marking out the way to the promise of God. He had to move from well to well and from difficulty, rejection and jealousy until he came into a place where ownership of them was not contended. Until he found the place where he could live and worship God in peace. He did not add to the offence. He did not stand up for his rights. He displayed gentleness.

Very often we discover God in times of adversity because it drives us closer to Him. Opposition is our opportunity to grow in godliness and 'become fruitful in the land'.

> *God is faithful and He will order our circumstances and get us to the right place at the right time. He will fulfil His promises and purposes for us – with our sensitivity, trust, co-operation and right attitude. Guard your well - your heart - for out of it flow the issues of life.*

Check it out: Gen 21:25-31, Gen 26:15-25, Jn 7:38, Prov 4:23

When The Anointing Comes Into The House

MARTHA AND MARY

LK 10:38-42

A very familiar story about two sisters. We can easily miss the significance because we know the passage so well. Yet we'll see as we unpack these few verses that sometimes our very gifts, talents and 'service to the Lord' can be used amiss and get in the way of a meaningful relationship with God.

On this particular occasion Jesus and His disciples were travelling and ministering and they arrived at Bethany, east of Jerusalem. They came into the village where scripture says that a certain woman called Martha welcomed Jesus into her home. Her gift of kindly hospitality began to flow. It's possible that some of the disciples came in too. Great emphasis was placed on hospitality in this culture, looking after guests was important and showed honour. This was Martha operating in a gift of service and there was much to be done to satisfy the needs of tired, hungry travelling ministers.

Martha's sister Mary was there to help her of course, but where was she! Martha turned around to find her and discovered that Mary was 'listening to the Lord's word, seated at His feet'.

What was going on here! You see, the Anointing had come into the house! Mary had given place to the anointing. Her position at the feet of Jesus was one of worship. She had recognised the need to make her relationship with the Lord a priority. She was calm and at peace in her spirit because her spirit was drawing from the Spirit of the Lord. The Lord's word here, is just conversation, but it was spirit to spirit and it would lead to a deepening of the relationship between Jesus and Mary, and from that, revelation would start to flow. Jesus said elsewhere in scripture that His food was to do the will of His Father, and He was feeding Mary through His words.

In other words, Mary was giving her full attention to the Word, Martha was giving her full attention to the works.

We're told Martha was *"distracted with all the preparations"*. She was weighed down with care as she went about her 'much service' for the Lord. Her practical desire to meet needs was becoming flustered and tainted and her peace was being eroded with care. She came up to Jesus and began to complain. Have you ever seen someone who is 'serving' but makes sure everyone knows about it!

102

When our feathers get ruffled we can have a tendency to try to make others responsible for our shortcomings. When we become agitated, we become irrational and short-sighted. Martha had failed to connect to the Anointing.

Let me tell you that schedules, plans, prejudices, traditions, timings – will all get knocked for six when the Anointing comes into the house. Do you want more of God! Are you prepared for what that means! It actually means that He will increase and you will decrease. *You* won't actually be the one in charge. Are you ok with that! Mary started out with a welcome and what she thought was a desire to provide hospitality. She *of course* wanted Jesus to come into her home – but in so doing she came face to face with herself as areas of weakness in her began to be exposed.

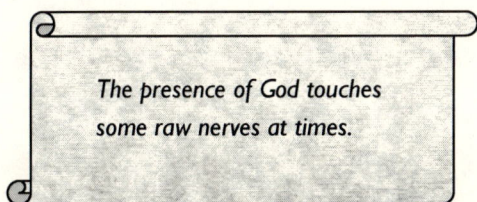

> The presence of God touches some raw nerves at times.

'There's work to be done and where's my sister? Tell her to help me Lord – or don't you care about that?' No emotional blackmail here then.

V41 – But the Lord answered her, *"Martha, Martha, you are worried and bothered about so many things"*. What began as compassion, concern, desire to serve was turning into bitterness and resentment. Martha was throwing a fit and really getting into the flesh.

Beware perfectionism and the intolerance that comes with it. It doesn't like its orderly programme being upset. Jesus said, 'There's truly only one thing that's important and of real benefit here and Mary has recognised that'.

'She's connected with the Anointed One and His Anointing. Her heart is to fellowship with Me and that won't be taken away from her'.

Jesus, the Christ, the Anointed One and His Anointing came into the house. When the anointing of God is around things happen. There's a shaking, a stirring, a separating, a dividing that goes on – of flesh and spirit.

By the way, there's another passage of scripture that gives further insight into these two sisters, where we read of the death and raising to life again of their brother Lazarus. Both women loved the Lord. He was their friend but again it seems that Martha had insecurities that clouded her spiritual insight and faith in her relationship with the Lord.

The two sisters have very different responses, perspectives and attitudes. Both with issues and areas of brokenness in their lives. One looking at a situation through fleshly eyes, the other wise enough to seek godly counsel and a deeper walk with God.

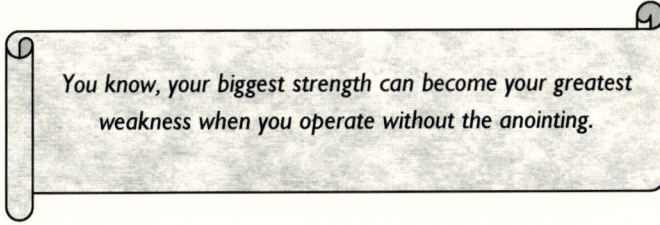

> *You know, your biggest strength can become your greatest weakness when you operate without the anointing.*

Galatians 5 talks about how we live life and the attitudes that are produced without the Spirit of God flowing through us. Martha's frustration meant that her 'well' (heart) became polluted with resentment, bitterness, envy, accusation, anger, strife.

Mary's hunger wasn't for natural food. Her desire was to be in the presence of her God, where the anointing was flowing. Close to the heart of Jesus.

WHAT THE ANOINTING BRINGS INTO OUR LIVES
Peace
Mary found rest for her spirit, soul and body in the presence of holiness. Peace that is spiritual and eternal, not hollow, fickle or shallow. Nothing missing, nothing broken. The wholeness kind of peace.

Revelation

From relationship comes intimacy comes revelation. Mary listened to words of life and something was imparted to her spirit. Deep calling to deep. You don't get that through a five-minute conversation.

Healing

The Healer - it's a part of who Jesus is – the Healer of our broken spirits, broken lives, broken dreams, broken bodies, Restorer of hope, Lifter of our heads, the Ointment poured out on our emotional scars and wounds, the Lover of our souls.

Deliverance

There's another place in scripture where we see someone sitting at the feet of Jesus – the demoniac that had been delivered of a legion of demons. Loosed by the authority of the Anointed One and His Anointing, he was clothed and in his right mind. Free. The anointing destroys yokes and bondages and heavy burdens. His deliverance led to his devotion.

UNBRIDLED

Are *you* prepared for the anointing to invade your house – your world – your circumstances! Have you ever fully allowed the Holy Spirit to come close and shake, train, mould, shape and fill you so that those things that keep you away from Jesus can be removed.

Even your 'works of service' can take on greater priority than your relationship with the Lord Jesus. He was always looking for relationship, not religion. It's not the works that the Lord is after, it's your heart. Service flows out of a heart that is His.

He wants you to leave father, mother, brother, sister – the things of the flesh – and cleave to Him, so that your spirit and His may become one and so that you can become unbridled in His service. Free to be all that He designs and purposes for you to be. Equipped for glory. Being joined to the Lord is a journey of becoming 'one'.

These are urgent days and the Lord is longing for you to walk in the holiness and the glory of God. He wants you free so that you can move out under the anointing with a passion for Jesus – radical, militant, unbridled love that desires to know Jesus personally and intimately.

The Lord is unbridling you and removing blinkers and giving you a hunger for Him and for His Kingdom. He longs and watches over you jealously and for the souls that have yet to find Him. He wants His Bride to take her place beside Him and step into the destinies and callings He has gifted you with.

The difference between Martha and Mary! Martha was preparing for a visitation from Jesus. Mary was preparing for a habitation. *She wanted Him to stay.* How about you! Where's the Church looking when Jesus is in the house! He enters offering us His heart – and looking for ours. He's the Great Lover and He has created us for relationship with Him.

THE BRIDE UNBRIDLED

We know that the Body of Christ is called the Bride. A bride is someone about to be married or newly married. A bride has a passionate, joyful, youthful, responsive, innocent love. She is in preparation for a coming together, a joining together, a separating from and a making of one where there were two.

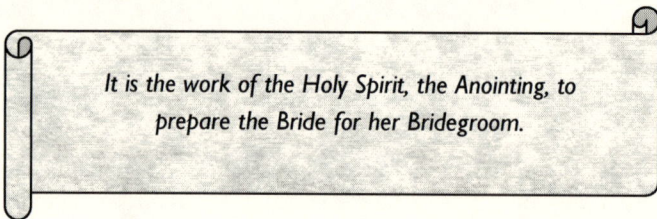

> *It is the work of the Holy Spirit, the Anointing, to prepare the Bride for her Bridegroom.*

Into my thoughts came a picture of a horse that has a controlling apparatus on its head. It curbs or restrains movement. Its head is thrown back by the hand pulling on the apparatus, which is the bridle. It's something that governs behaviour and response. A young horse needs 'breaking in' so that it becomes trained in submission and is restrained or prevented from being both wayward and potentially dangerous through the wrong use of its power.

You know, a horse contains a whole lot of power but if left to run rampant that power can kill somebody.

There is a process, a programme, a strategy employed in teaching a horse to be responsive to its master so that rider and animal function in cooperation with one another. So that both give and receive the best service, partnership and benefit.

Hear this analogy with your spiritual ears. There comes a time when the horse becomes so responsive and familiar with the ways of its master, where trust and relationship have developed, and a maturity has taken place, that that apparatus can be removed from its head and the horse will willingly move in response to its master's voice and promptings and will walk along by his side unbridled and unrestrained.

The Lord says 'I have been preparing My Bride to take her place by Me and walk with me without restraint. Your heart will know Me, My ways, My voice and respond to Me with freedom and desire to serve Me, please Me, step out with Me into the destinies and callings I have prepared, trained and equipped you for in these strategic days'.

'My desire is to unbridle you in the sense of being without the restraint and restriction of all that has held you back. Allow your hearts to respond with deep love to the promptings of My Holy Spirit, for as many as are led by the Spirit of God are the sons of God. I am leading you and calling you My Bride to follow the Anointing and work with Me in these end times'.

'A Bride longs for and desires her husband. I am stirring and quickening and awakening desires in you to thirst for Me, to long for Me, to seek Me, to worship Me, to come with Me and take your place at such a time as this in my end-time purposes for the Church and the nations, for yes there are those of you that I have called to the nations to minister in My Name'.

'As the Father has loved Me, so have I loved you – will you respond to Love! My plans are not to harm you but to give you hope and a future. Will you allow Me to set you free to be all that I know and purpose for you to be! Will you respond to the Anointing coming into *your* house?'

Anointing

Winning Ways

CONTENTMENT

I Tim 6:6 – "Godliness... is a means of great gain, when accompanied by contentment.."

God says that He has set us apart for His purposes. In scripture, the word sanctified means just that, like a priest set apart for holy purposes.

Godliness is having godly or holy behaviour, motives and attitudes, being like God in character. That, together with being satisfied and quietly happy with whatever is going on in your life, good or bad, is absolutely to your advantage. It's a means of success and victory when you can keep your head as everyone else around you is losing theirs! If you can act in the same manner that God would, with peace and restraint, curbing the desire to complain, even experiencing deep-down quietness of heart, then you're on a winner! This is someone not governed by circumstances.

God is saying here that having contentment is worth more than you could ever possess materially.

It's of far greater value to live life with that inner satisfaction, from a character that has the God-given ability to look beyond the 'now' and focus on something of higher worth.

The opposite leads to dissatisfaction, frustration, resentment, anger, ungodly and fleshly thinking that steals our joy. We always have a choice – life or death. God says – choose life!

SECRETS OF SUCCESS

Phil 4:4-13. Look at the progression in these verses. Paul had made these things a lifestyle. As you read these verses, Who comes to mind? Gentle, joyful, mild-mannered, not anxious, over-wrought or uneasy. Not fearful, agitated, apprehensive or stressed out. Committing everything and everyone to prayer with the earnest expectation and assurance that God would respond. Experiencing in all these things the absolute peace, steadfastness and immovability of God. Quietness and confidence as His strength. Surely this is a picture of Jesus! He knew freedom in His emotions from every disturbance. He didn't allow fickle feelings to dominate Him. He let a state of calm bypass His thoughts and stand guard over His heart and mind. In other words, His soulish responses were kept in check.

How? It's where you allow your mind to settle. Verse eight would be a good one to commit to memory.

What sets you up to get you upset? It's stinking thinking. This verse will keep you on track to maintaining your cool.

"True" – faithful, constant, trustworthy, genuine, righteous

"Noble" or *"Honourable"* – high in rank and character, exalted, excellent

"Just" or *"Right"* – fair, impartial

"Pure" – clean, without impediment, unconditional

"Lovely" – admirable, delightful, worthy of love, beautiful, valuable, commendable

"Good Report" or *"Repute"* – truth, positive, best, highest, edifying, character-building

Plenty to think about! Paul meditated on these things. Meditate means to mutter, murmur, muse, whisper, reflect, thoughtfully consider, contemplate, give serious thought to. He chewed these things over and over until they became a lifestyle. In doing this, Paul was actually paying attention to the very attributes of God Himself. He was totally absorbed with the things of God and so could live on a higher plane than that of reacting without self-control.

V9 – Paul says 'this is how I live my life and how I succeed. What you see true of me, do it and be it.' Find a mentor, someone who is beyond where you are in the faith. Watch them and imitate them.

V12 – How did Paul get to this level? He learned it. By life's experiences, its ups and downs, it's good and bad. Through these things, he learnt how to master the flesh and trust God. It had caused Paul to have great moral responsibility towards others, demonstrated in the way he lived his life.

God's Word says that Jesus *"'learned' obedience ... by the things He suffered" (Phil 2:8).*

Paul's life was so given over to God that he could say *"for me to live is Christ and to die is gain" (Phil 1:21).* Either way he was a winner. Perhaps not a more contented man in the bible. Why ? He knew what it was to have little, he knew what it was to have plenty. He knew not to rely on either *(Phil 4:11-12).*

From brutal and zealous to gentle and zealous, Paul's life underwent a radical change once he encountered Jesus Christ. It changed his entire outlook. Step by step along a pathway of difficulty, suffering a catalogue of disasters, he never lost his tenacity. **God doesn't change our personality, He deals with our character.** Paul 'learnt' how to change his thoughts and attitudes until he could sing praises in the dungeon of darkness and be glad in the hour of hunger. He says to you – things you have seen and learnt of me – imitate!

Build them into your character until they become a way of life, and every bit as much a challenge to others.

Check it out : Ps 131:1-2, 2 Cor 11:24-28

I give you My WORD

In the beginning was the Word, and the Word was with God, and the Word was God

Jn 1

WORDSONGS

2

WORDSONGS

Why WORDSONGS?

The Psalms (poems) were written to be sung to the accompaniment of music. They are the Word of God in song and carry great power, authority and anointing.

Try singing one out loud until faith springs up in you. Better still, how about writing your own Psalm of Praise as a personal testimony to the faithfulness of God? That's exactly what David did so often during his sheep-tending years in the desert and those psalms are a spiritual journal; memorial stones for him to reflect upon at times when his soul needed encouraging.

Each one reveals the heart of the writer, and the heart of God. No punches are pulled. Joy, sorrow, failure, life, death – all life's experiences are portrayed in the songs of scripture. These things are recorded as examples for us to learn what works, and what most certainly doesn't.

All Change

Sitting in a railway carriage on my way to town,

Studied all the serious faces wearing each a frown.

Every day the same monotonous routines;

A life which lacks variety, least that's the way it seems.

We long for something different, but don't you find it strange

At the utter panic we incur when someone mentions 'change'.

We find security in sameness, so immediately we tut,

But secretly then realise our lives are in a rut.

Some things are constant and immutable, it's true

But change is all around us and affects much that we do.

We say we're working late tonight and then the family find,

They've eaten early, we appear, because we've 'changed' our mind.

Last Sunday folk discovered we weren't somehow quite so sweet.

In church we had to 'change' our place, someone sitting in our seat!

'Just for a change' we'll drive another route today,

And 'that'll make a change' are things we often say.

The living room's a mess and nothing can be found,
It's Spring, so whilst we're at it, we'll 'change' it all around!
Things going on around us, shake our security
Thank God for Jesus, in Him such constancy.

When God saw all those serious faces frowning in their sin,
His Son was sent, a radical, to 'change' our lives through Him.
He simply took some water and 'changed' it into wine
And through God's Word we learn He is a timely Sign.

For He was sent to 'change' each heart of stone
And blood He shed did for everyone atone.
If we would grow more like Him through all the passing days,
Know what? We need to change our strong and wilful ways.

For on the Cross His work once done,
"It's finished" was His sigh –
One day before Him 'changed' we'll be
In the twinkling of an eye.

Sitting in a railway carriage I suddenly found it strange –
I realised I'd passed my stop, as the guard called out, "All change! "
And instead of wishing 'change' would come to everyone else I see,
I sent a silent prayer to God: "Let 'change' begin – in me! "

Allowed To Be Me

Some days it seems everything around

Is meant for harm, to bring me down

And just the fact that I'm breathing air

Seems to cause offence, man that's hard to bear.

Someone trying to manipulate

Attempting to control,

Put out if I won't co-operate,

Destroying my very soul.

I know in every situation

I won't please, meet expectation,

But I want so much to hear you say

Some encouraging word to make my day.

Hope deferred sickens the heart

Yet love and kindness would blow me apart.

Sometimes instead of selfish desire,

Couldn't you care what I might require?

Couldn't you ask before you assume,

Consider me instead of presume?

So Father…

Here I am and what am I doing,

What is my purpose here?

Groping in the darkness,

Won't You help me to see things clear.

Yet, I'm allowed to be me

For You've made me the way I am.

I look through Your eyes

And then realise

I'm allowed to be me,

You let me be me,

It's all right to be me,

I'm allowed to be … me.

An Angel's Tear

I dreamt that there was moment when I caught an angel's tear.

So clear, the words He spoke to me –

"This is your Saviour, come, draw near."

Standing in my vision in the midst of heaven's celebration,

Thousands of the heavenly host singing to their God.

Myriads of angels lost in worship of their King,

Yet looking down upon the earth and wondering,

What praises have the saints to bring?

"Look child, see the scars upon His brow,

Broken heart exalted now.

Body changed but scars allow

You saint, to know your God, and bow."

He took my hand and spoke again.

"Gaze upon bruised feet and hands,

No words required to understand

That God completed His deepest plans,

Evidenced by blood on Jesus' hands."

The Lord's salvation given free

In cruel death and agony.

Do His children celebrate the victory

Of life redeemed at Calvary?

The Lord, ascended high

Yet I heard the heavens loudly sigh.

I thought I saw an angel cry

As he sadly asked the Master – "Why?"

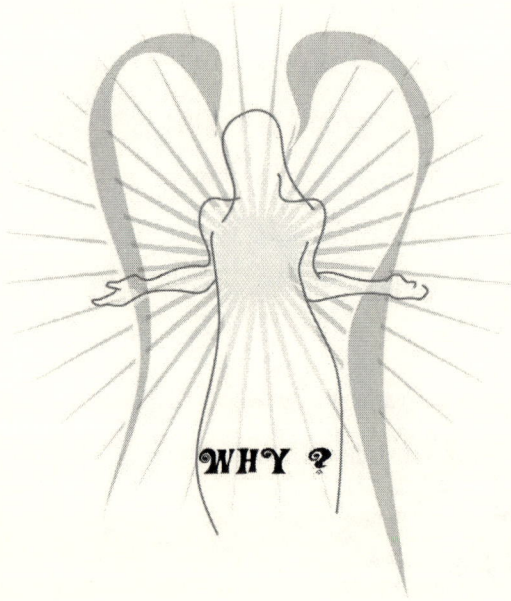

WHY ?

Beneath My Feet

It's wet today,

Had to sleep in the underground.

My cardboard dugout's soaked you see

And I simply would've drowned.

Found some butts to puff on –

Well, it whiled away the time.

Listened to some buskers

Playing blues, with dance and mime.

There's no-one keeping score of me,

How many swigs I take

And walking in the park is free –

I just really need a break.

It's nice in Spring

When grass is green and there's flowers at my feet.

I often sit on the old park bench

And beg a bite to eat.

I'm looked upon as 'down and out'

But it sometimes seems to me,

That many folks in city suits

Are more depressed than me!

Yeah, it's hard at times without a home,

Society's not always kind,

But I get by and life is mine

To take it as I find.

There's those with house and job and car

With burdens to the ground,

And I wonder who would rather have

The space and peace I've found.

I tramp along the roads at morn

And hear the sounds of birds,

And the sun's awakening at dawn —

Treasures in the seen and heard.

All kinds of mingling folk I see

Along a city street,

A simple life with pleasure rare

Is all beneath my feet.

The cold and hardship I endure

And pity you can keep,

For when the sun is red in sky,

With real friends do I sleep.

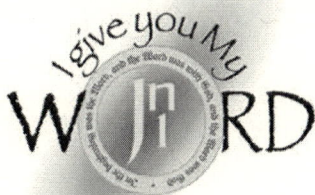

Colours

A canvas spreads before us

The moment we are born

And the colours of our lifetime,

Images will form.

That which we create

Takes shape before our eyes.

A picture can be beautiful

Or fill our hearts with sighs.

Maturity is born of years,

Experience the same.

Ensure in all the living

That happiness remains.

Let the colours that you paint

Enrich the lives of many,

So as you glimpse across the years

Your enemies aren't any.

Colour a life with good things,

Paint a heart of care,

And attract as does a magnet,

Friends who are glad you're there.

Daddy's Girl

I always thought when I was young
There was all the time in the world,
With endless rounds of parties and fun,
Colours and shapes that unfurled.

Then, as a child, I saw as a child
With everything always so bright.
I never knew that life would reveal
Sadness that seems dark as night.

I always saw such a future of happiness,
Love and a warm caress,
Chestnuts, and snowflakes and cosy log fires.
Holiday places and bright smiling faces.

Tumbling streams,
Oh such simple desires.
I always thought I'd have you forever,
The love and the warmth of a family together.

I reach in my mind,

Precious memories to find.

All the time in the world,

For me to be daddy's own girl.

All the time in the world,

To appreciate family as well.

What happened – to all the time in the world?

I miss you daddy.

Footnote :

Let my life always point you to Jesus,

Tho' sometimes things happen, that don't always please us.

Time's running out,

Of that there's no doubt.

God's calling us from our sin,

Eternity beckoning with Him.

All the time, all the time,

All the time,

In God's world.

While there's still time, won't you reach out and let Him come *into* **your** *life?*

EX Factor!

Let me try to **EX**press, let me state, let me say

You're the **EX**pert God, the One who knows the way.

Let me put it clear, let me be **EX**act,

You're just spot-on perfect as a matter of fact.

I **EX**alt Your Name, yeah I lift You high

Cos You're **EX**ceptional God and I'll tell You why.

You **EX**ceed, surpass, You're more than enough,

EXtravagant love and all that stuff.

You're **EX**cellent God in all Your ways

And I give to You **EX**uberant praise.

Respect!

I got **EX**pectations and an eager longing

To **EX**perience, prove, the joy of belonging.

EXtraordinary **EX**ploits I'm gonna do

EXpanding my horizons because of You.

Your love and Your mercy are always **EX**treme

Overflowing, **EX**cessive, You know what I mean?

My hands I raise, yeah to You **EX**tend,

No **EX**cuse, I'll praise You to the very end.

Respect!

EXquisite

Foolish Wisdom

Why did You call *me* Lord?

I see no sense in it.

Foolish wisdom,

Foolish plan.

'Go into all the world' You said,

Foolish wisdom,

Foolish plan.

Why did You choose *me* Lord?

I see no sense in it.

Foolish wisdom,

Foolish plan.

I laughed and mocked You, looked with scorn,

Foolish wisdom,

Foolish man.

He Gave Me You

O Lord I sighed, O Lord I cried,

I'm feeling crushed on every side.

I'm not fulfilled, I'm all alone,

How lonely seems a silent 'phone.

Verbally I've been abused,

And my emotions now are bruised.

What can I do, who'll see me through –

He gave me you.

So many problems at my door,

A ringing bell, is that one more?

My tension mounts, I'm feeling stressed,

Who's there for me when I'm hard pressed?

Not a second of my own

With others living in my home,

Where is there space, yet in this zoo –

He gave me you.

You hear my heart, my silent plea,
You understand the needs in me.
Just to be heard, it matters much,
And as you pass, a gentle touch
Tells me that you've recognised
The agony in my tired eyes.
This contact grew, until I knew –
He gave me you.

Support is there and tender care
And loyalty beyond compare.
You ease my pain, you take the strain,
Your wisdom is refreshing rain.
Suddenly I've confidence
I'm more relaxed and not so tense,
For here's a friend, not perfect, true –
But He gave me ... you.

Heart to Heart

Communication is not a problem when words are spoken from the heart,
Silence sometimes speaking deeper truth than loudest words impart.
If man would take the time to learn another's long-closed mind,
Then peace between brothers could be the greatest treasured find.

And feelings hidden from the world could more freely be expressed
As open hearts encourage more joy and peace and rest.
In all of life we seek to learn still newer, better ways
But progress would be faster in understanding what each to other says.

To listen is a virtue, a gift sometimes in life quite rare,
But hearing words *un*spoken is the secret of greatest care.
To see and hear the deep-felt needs that lie within a man,
To offer self and offer time is surely life's great plan.

To seek a soul that understands and meets such basic need,
To find a heart that's wise enough to trust, is joy indeed.
For wisdom of the world is changing every careless day,
But rich the one who finds a Friend to guide along the way.

Is It Me In Need?

You say you've got good news for me
But I'm kinda confused
Cos all I see is lethargy
So I'm somewhat bemused.

You explain the shortness of the hour
Is that fiction – or fact?
There seems to be a lack of power
In the way you look and act.

You say it's true, that there's no doubt
That Jesus came to save.
Well, shouldn't you then raise a shout
If new life He really gave?

I'm looking for an answer see,
Have you got one to give?
Have *you* got such reality
In the life you daily live?

Didn't He mix with those in need
And heal their sick and blind,
Didn't He live by word *and* deed,
Are you bearing that in mind?

See – I've got problems of my own,
I need to know the way.
If you hadn't 've said, I'd never have known
That Christ is yours today.

What difference *does* He make to you,
What *are* you offering me?
Cos in the world, you know it's true,
There's *enough* of misery!

Jesus said *"I came that they might have life, and might have it abundantly"*
(Jn 10:10).

It Was Good Man

The Spirit of God hovered over the earth,

He looked and saw its potential, its worth.

He brooded over a void dark as night

And poured out His Spirit calling "Let there be light!"

And it was good, it was very good,

It lit up the blackness around.

The dark He called night and in a wonderful way

The light and the night formed the very first day.

Then God said "Let the vapours part

To divide the skies, it's what's on My heart.

Let the waters below become as seas

And dry land form with plants and trees."

And it was good, it was very good,

As He set each star in the sky,

With sun and moon both shining bright

It filled God's heart with joy and delight.

He filled the seas with fish as He pleased
And birds flew through the air with ease.
Cattle and reptiles filled the land
And God was thrilled with the work of His hand.

God carried out His great heart plan
In creating from dust the body of man.
He breathed His life into every bone
And He was pleased with what He'd done.

He gave to man everything displayed,
As companion He created a maid.
Together they would subdue the land
And worship God walking hand in hand.

As God surveyed all that was done,
His heart was glad and His rest was won.
The seventh day was one of rest
Declared as holy and by the Lord well blessed.

Creation reveals God's master plan,
Eternal fellowship with the heart of man.
He looked and saw everything was good –
But man, in all his foolishness, just never understood.

Check it out : Gen 1 : 1-31, Gen 2 : 1-4, 7

Love Affair

Prayer,

A love affair

Between my God and I.

Caring, sharing, bearing,

Knowing God as Father.

Pouring out my inmost heart,

Enjoying special moments,

Secret times set apart.

Not stifled or robbed

In the clutter of the day

But certain God's beside me

Hearing every word I say.

Setting free my spirit to praise and glorify,

He never misses my whisper or ignores my heartfelt sigh.

Being privileged to carry

Everything to God in prayer,

Anytime and anywhere, my Father's everywhere.

Walking in the countryside,

The sight, the sounds, the smells,

Every shape and colour

Of their Creator yells,

And I can offer thanks

As the wind blows in the trees.

A butterfly or sweet birdsong

Can bring me to my knees.

At home, abroad, friends, family,

As needs are brought to mind,

I simply give them back to Him

Until release I find.

Then there are times when I am still,

To hear His Spirit speak.

His voice, His Word, refreshes me

As I direction seek.

My spirit and my senses

Are all involved in prayer,

Speaking with my Father

A prayerful love affair.

Because of Jesus and the Cross

We're reconciled as one,

And prayer is a relationship

With Father, Spirit, Son.

Prayer

Mat 6 : 6 "But when you pray, go into your inner room, and when you have shut your door, pray to your Father who is in secret, and your Father who sees in secret will repay you."

More Hugs

To say I'm there, to say I care,

To understand, to lend a hand.

To say it doesn't matter when you fail,

To give you strength when you're feeling frail.

To say "I know", to convey that I'm aware,

To encourage, love, give a squeeze

To share, to know, to put at ease.

To warm, to cause to smile, to allow a tear,

To massage pain, dispel a fear.

To say there's someone by your side,

To sometimes be a place to hide.

To express a friendship's special touch,

To say you're loved so very much.

To give you confidence to do,

To help unfold the hidden you.

To say you're missed when you're away,

To let you know you're thought of every day.

To be the arms of God above,

The tangible expression of His love.

To comfort, support and reassure,

These are the things a hug is for.

4 each day for survival
8 each day for maintenance
12 each day for growth

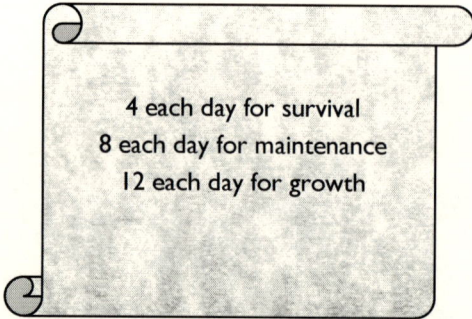

See also "Hugs: Pass Them On" in WORDTHOUGHTS)

No Greater Love

You've known all along what's in my heart,

The darkness that's lurking there.

There's not a thing that's hidden from your careful sight,

Not a sin, not a doubt, not a care.

You're sensitive to the things going on,

You know what I'm going through.

You're feeling with me, You know all along,

Every thought, every deed that I do.

Always beside me each second I live,

Working Your perfect plan.

There's no greater love than the love that You give,

As You reach out Your nail-pierced hand.

All that I've seen when I've recognised sin,

Is all that You've known all along

And yet You remain the truest of Friends

When You could have deserted and gone.

In my failings I figure it's best that I go,

In my reason that's what I believe,

Yet whenever I try to walk away,

My side You simply won't leave.

There are times when I've tried to run and hide,

For such powerful love numbs my mind,

For instead of condemning, your smile's all I see,

From a heart that is loving and kind.

Then I suddenly hear that the sound of Your voice

Isn't harsh as I think it might be,

But You're gentle and patient, faithful and good

In all of Your dealings with me.

Can't really imagine what life just might be

If You were not there by my side.

You've given me hope and such confidence,

In my welfare You take such great pride.

You show me acceptance and loyalty,

What more could You possibly give,

And I'll never find greater friendship and love

In all of the years that I live.

144

Shammah

On a day when it seems no-one is there to care, not a soul on my side, no friendly face to turn to. When it's dark and it's lonely and it seems so cold outside – who is there to run to, who'll show me what to do ?

And then I hear ...

> "Jehovah, Shammah,
>
> I'm the God who's always there,
>
> The ageless and eternal One
>
> I'm timeless in my care
>
> I am Shammah – there with you.
>
> The Everlasting One
>
> Eternal and true
>
> Shammah,
>
> **I AM** – is close by you. "

At a time when I'm completely on my own.

So lost and afraid, my world just falling round me.

I cry and I call out, "Is there anyone who'll hear,

Who is there to lean on, who'll be a friend to me? "
And then I hear . . .

"Jehovah, Shammah,

I'm the God who's always there,

The ageless and eternal One,

I'm timeless in my care,

I am Shammah – there with you.

The everlasting One

Eternal and true

Shammah,

I AM – is close by you."

And Shammah – I AM – is close by you!

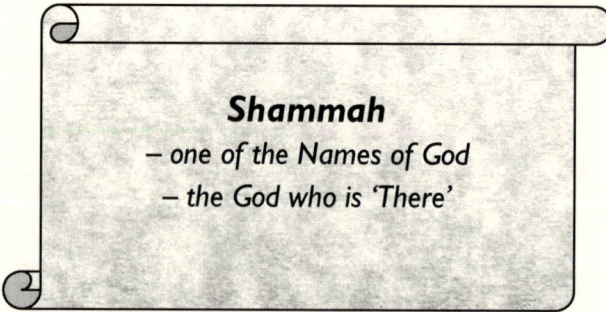

Shammah
– one of the Names of God
– the God who is 'There'

Song Of The Wilderness

Pillar of cloud by day

Pillar of fire by night

So many signs along the way

Of Your heavenly provision –

In the wilderness

Never leaving Your children alone

Guiding to a land of blessing.

Supernatural in Your care,

Protective in Your presence.

Like them I've often seemed lost along the way,

Often apt to go astray

Yet every time You've found me

And set me on my feet.

Manna from heaven,

Bread of life so sweet

Help me to see You,
Help me to believe and trust,
Help me to recognise
Your footprints in the dust.
Help me to sing a song –
In the wilderness

Lord of the wilderness,
Lord of the wilderness,
Lead me to your land of rest
As I sing to you my song –
As I worship all day long –
Even –
In the wilderness

Suddenly

Suddenly,

You're the God of 'suddenly.'

When it seems that there's no way

And hopes are shattered day by day,

In Your time You do it very 'suddenly.'

Suddenly,

You're the God of 'suddenly.'

No impossibility,

Just an opportunity,

For You to work a miracle,

Glory to You Lord!

The above are words to which a friend later added music and is one of the tracks on a recording entitled 'Relentless Love.'

See 'God Of Suddenly' in WORDSEARCH

Teardrop Isle

Beautiful teardrop isle,

Jewelled pendant in a shimmering blue ocean.

Regal palms waving their greeting,

Clear azure sky and tropical sun.

Sweet fragrant incense, aromatic spices,

Colourful flowers.

A Paradise Creation

All around me.

The ocean roaring its applause,

Fruits from a Garden of Eden.

Ancient traditions, timeless cultures,

A galaxy of sights, sounds, smells.

Blessings plentiful and abundant.

Peace and serenity invading the senses.

Was this how it was meant to be?

The Promise

"Still the night, holy the night, all is calm, all is bright."

All is *calm*, all is *still*! The words hang heavily amidst the hustle and
bustle of a turning world.
What is Christmas, if it isn't parties, feasts and drink –
Shopping, presents, cards and very little time to think!

All caught up with working out our tiny little plans,
If anything, we'd gladly use *another* pair of hands!
The stress our treadmill lives seem daily to endure,
Diseases that we suffer from and seem to find no cure.

Earthquake, famine, war and every kind of plague,
What are our lives now seemingly so empty and so vague?
We're working hard to pay our way and live our lives with ease,
Yet we forget our fellow man with all *his* many needs,

Ah yes, but it's Christmas now, a time to celebrate,
But is there any future hope, or is it all too late?

Thank God it wasn't in the tumult or the earthquake that He came,
But through the door of human life in quietness proclaimed.
Quite naturally you'll find Him if you take the time to look,
Jesus here beside you, though the earth it never shook.

In the midst of human suffering, of tragedy and fear,
In sorrow and in poverty you'll find Emmanuel near.
The King whose gifts are life and peace and glory yet to come,
Brings comfort to believing hearts and hope of future home.

> All your Spirit promised
> All the Father willed,
> Now these eyes behold it
> Perfectly fulfilled.

The promise of the Father's heart
Is with us every day,
There's hope contained in holy flesh
The Life, the Truth, the Way.

A promise needs to be believed,
The Gift just has to be received.
All *is* calm, all *is* bright
If you can see beyond the clamour God's eternal Light.

Lk 1 : 31-32a "And behold you will conceive in your womb, and bear a son, and you shall name Him Jesus. He will be great, and will be called the Son of the Most High."

The Sands Of Time

The tide goes out, and then comes in.

Sometimes gently,

Sometimes in great billowing waves

Crashing upon the shore.

Each ebb of the sea cleansing, disinfecting,

Removing waste and debris.

Nature faithfully extracting poison

And that which mars what was unspoilt beauty.

In its place golden crystals, a beach carpet,

Safe, soft underfoot,

Comforting, welcoming, inviting.

A place where treasures can be deposited,

Discovered and marvelled at all over again.

Such is the love of God,

And such is the memory of friendship

That holds the heart close.

The Weakest Link

In my heart is a dull lonely ache,

Feeling wretched through things said and done.

There's no lower a place I could sink

Than to take out my hurt on someone.

Disjointed, bewildered, bemused,

Let down by the one you believed in.

My anger has left you confused

And my grief is the sorrow of sin.

Incomplete without your forgiveness

The hours passing painfully by.

Never would I willing hurt you,

That I did I cannot deny.

Harshness has caused you to go

Wounded, into your shell.

My remorse is more than you know,

More than I easily can tell.

Never wanted to do or to be
The things that did manifest.
What I truly want you to see
Is that which will leave you blessed.

That I love you I hope you believe,
That you've grace to forgive is my plea.
My repentance you'll somehow receive
For I know that the fault lay in me.

I will hope in the God who still loves me
When there's no lower a place I can sink,
I will call to the Father above me,
Make me strong at my weakest link.

Rom 7 : 18-19

When Darkness Fell

I could never understand the accusation,
I was at a loss to see the reason or the rhyme.
The atrocity He was accused on didn't make sense to me –
The punishment just didn't fit the 'crime'.

Assigned to special duty I kept the closest guard,
The crowd abusive to the end.
I watched Him beaten, suffering, spat upon
And wondered, did this man have but one friend?

His clothes were stripped away from Him,
His body torn and bruised.
With cruel thorns that pierced His brow,
I feared that this was Innocence accused.

The intensity of His gaze met mine
Though He never spoke a word.
When nails His hands and feet did pierce,
Not a cry from Him was heard.

How could it be – no oaths, no vengeance and no curse,

No spite nor blasphemy.

The utmost agony and pain

Yet such humility.

And when those eyes reached to the crowd

He called "Forgive them Father true,

Don't hold this sin against them

For they know not what they do."

And then He seemed to breathe His last,

With a breaking heart He sighed,

And darkness fell upon the land

As a Saviour bled and died.

It was at that moment dark and still

My blinded eyes did see

That this was truly the Son of God

Who'd suffered there for me.

And with the shame of all my sin,

With the greatest sense of loss,

I knelt and gave my life to One

Who'd given His upon that Cross.

Father,

forgive them.

You Fit My Life So Well

You are the centre of my world,

You fit my life so well.

Where I was just an empty shell,

Much more than any hope or dream,

Much more than I could tell,

You fit my life so well,

You fit my life so well.

Through all the moments sweet and sad,

Through all the good, through all the bad,

Your love will keep me strong,

Will be my portion and my song,

You fit my life so well,

You fit my life so well.

Without You

When it seemed that I was on my own

Just wandering and feeling so alone,

My Jesus saw it all.

When trying to remember love,

Acceptance reached me from above,

When on my way to finish all,

My Jesus heard the faintest call.

A time of searching desperately,

My hopelessness reality,

Just running from the pain,

Life seemed lonely and so vain.

Then "Jesus loves you" said a voice,

"Jesus loves you, so make your choice."

A street-preacher man,

Bible-teacher man

Showed me the Saviour's face

And pointed me to grace.

My angry soul lashed out in fight
"Someone loves me? In this plight?"
Yet somehow in the darkest night
I learnt that I was precious in God's sight.

In the street, right then, I knelt
And received the love of God.
Defensiveness began to melt
As acceptance for the very first time I felt.

And He has kept me all these years,
Faithfulness and mercy have calmed my fears.
My Saviour's been my closest Friend,
The One on whom I really can depend.

He'll always be upon my mind
For, when there was no-one else to find,
My Jesus took me in.

He cleansed and made me whole,
Breathed peace into this soul.
My Jesus gave His life,
A willing sacrifice.

I knelt and looked to Calvary
And knew at last that I was free.
His blood has washed me white as snow,
Oh how I love my Jesus so.

A cruel tree
Became the way of life for me.

Jesus, I will always look to You,
For there's no life, no life at all
If it's not in You.
I'm so thankful to You Lord,
From a heart that's filled with love.
I'm so grateful to You Lord,
For your guidance and your peace,
For joy and such release,
For love and goodness too,
What would I do – without You?

This is the very real testimony experience of a friend who at the time was 18 years old, battling the abuse of alcoholism in her home. God can take what would break you and turn it into your testimony too.

WORDTHOUGHTS

3

WORDTHOUGHTS

Set aside some times outside of your normal routine when you can be quiet and alone. Take with you pen and notepaper and just 'go be with God'. Simple as that. Do it at a time and place that will remain undisturbed. Whether you walk, drive out somewhere or shut yourself away – be creative.

Be incognito for that time – and allow your senses to appreciate whatever you have surrounded yourself with, using them as tools with which to communicate with God and Him with you. So many possibilities. So much variety. Times with the Lord need never be dull or boring because He isn't.

Taste - Perhaps an early breakfast or an afternoon tea with the Lord

Touch - An object, a flower, a precious possession that will focus your thoughts

Sight - Look around you and marvel at the presence of God

Hearing - Sounds of life that remind you of Him, music, nature

Smell - Fragrances everywhere – perfume, coffee, mown grass, flowers

Cool With God

"...if we are faithless, He remains faithful" 2 Tim 2:13

Remember the story of the tortoise and the hare? A race between two very unlikely opponents- the outcome almost a forgone conclusion.

Yet as we all know, it wasn't the speed or ability of the hare that won the prize – it was the consistency and commitment of the tortoise.

Nowadays, with our microwave mentality, faithfulness isn't a 'cool' word.   Honour, dependability, constancy versus fast turnover, overnight success and instant coffee!   Reliability, loyalty, and trustworthiness eclipsed by 'on-the-spot' marriages and quickie divorce.

Faithfulness, by very definition, is a lifestyle. It's costly. It doesn't seek a response. It focuses upon a long-term goal and moves towards it with unwavering fidelity. It is borne out of closeness and relationship, displayed in honesty and steadfastness and not swayed by adverse circumstances.

No-one will ever know how faithful you are until you have been with and served them over a period of time. Your life will eventually prove it.

Faithfulness is part of the unchanging nature of God. Portrayed in the life of Jesus throughout the gospels. A facet of Holy Spirit fruit and character.

Faithfulness is *very* cool with God!

Faithful

Daybreak Prayer

Well, I've done it. Here I am sitting outside, pen poised. I may have cut my finger whilst slicing lemon for my tea, I may have stubbed my toe on the parasol base as I stumbled sleepily into the garden – but I've done it – risen early to write - 6.00am to be precise!

Bleary-eyed I've wandered purposely around the different parts of the garden enjoying the slow assault on my senses. Traces of heady night-scented stock fill my nostrils, water trickles relentlessly from the fountain; the birdsong is sweet at this hour of the day. I see the watery sun peeking through the trees and watch the morning mist slowly clear. An acrobatic blue tit perches on the nuts just in front of me. A wood pigeon coos softly on top of a neighbour's chimney aerial.

They say the early bird catches the worm. Simple pleasures experienced at this morning watch that will be missed as the world awakens and the day begins in earnest. Stillness invades the surroundings, yet to be broken. I can already hear the distant drone of motorway traffic.

A breeze works it's way around my shoulders. The day promises to be hot again with temperatures in the high 80's. The scorched grass bears witness of a prolonged dry spell. I relish this post-dawn escape from heat and humidity. Enjoy each rainbow-hued dewdrop on grass and flowers before they disappear. A bee already at work collecting pollen. It's early. It's cool. Once again I look over to the fountain, that of a young girl catching water in a container which cascades to the bowls beneath. Is that a tear running down her cheek, or merely a smudge of dirt?

You say in Your Word Lord, "Be *still and know that I am God.*" I recognise Your handiwork all around. All these wondrous gems of creation shouting of You by their very existence. Still I long for You to walk with me and talk with me just as you did with Adam in the Garden of Eden. Talk to me before the daily noise drowns You and voices crowd You out. Before the demands of pressing routine invade the preciousness of a quiet time with You. Even the plane in the sky gatecrashes this tranquillity but for now I am at rest and seeking You. Create Your stillness within just as I enjoy it without. Let Your serenity and repose be mine. You are my God and I would commune with You.

The wispy clouds drift carefree in the azure sky. I look up as though searching for You. Soon I must enter the bustle of the day, but momentarily I am Yours alone. Deposit something of Your love within me – and let me be like that fountain, overflowing and bringing refreshment to others. Let there be a relentless trickle, no flow, of Your life coursing through my veins so that when others touch me, they touch Your heart. Or like a star in Your sky, let me reflect Your light and glory and as I step out into my world let this soul repose keep me connected with You. May the sweetness of these moments be precious memories that sustain me throughout the clamour of my day. And let my spirit always echo "Amen".

Ps 118 : 24   *"This is the day which the Lord has made; Let us rejoice and be glad in it".*

Hi Lord

Hi Lord, it's me sitting here once again before the day begins in earnest. I want to thank You that whilst I've slept, You have faithfully and diligently kept watch over the world. You held the stars in place during the night and caused them to shine brightly, calling each of them by name. You are intimate with Your Creation, involved to a degree that none of us anywhere near comprehends. You never slumber, You're always on the job. Anytime and anywhere I can call out to You – and You hear. You are 'Shammah' – the God Who is 'there'. Thank You Lord, that even when I am not yet fully awake, You are alert and watchful. My eyes are glazed, Yours are on the sparrow, and upon each of Your children. Your gaze is so intense it numbers the hairs on my head. You remind me that I can *never* escape from Your love. I cannot run from You. You surround and envelop me with such warm comfort.

I'm alone in the presence of my God, breathing the very life You have placed within me. I am known of You.

Hugs : Pass Them On

A hug conveys :-

Welcome, comfort, I'm glad to see you, I love you, I understand, come again, I care, I know how you feel, I've been there, I'm with you – and a thousand other emotions.

It brings warmth, reassurance, security, acceptance, inclusion. It shows the heart.

When a hug is with-held it denies someone any or all of these things.

Ever thought about a 'Ministry of Hugs? 'A channel for the Lord to love someone through you.

The world needs it.

You'll Never Walk Alone

The road of grief can sometimes be a dark journey. Keep walking and you will experience the softening of the darkness and the lessening of the pain.

This road shines brighter the longer it is walked upon until at journey's end, sorrow gives way to peace – and the discovery that you have not walked alone.

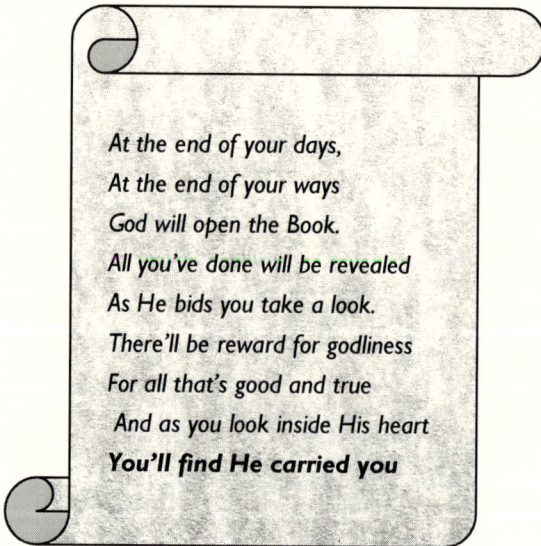

At the end of your days,
At the end of your ways
God will open the Book.
All you've done will be revealed
As He bids you take a look.
There'll be reward for godliness
For all that's good and true
And as you look inside His heart
You'll find He carried you

I give you my WORD

In the beginning was the Word, and the Word was with God, and the Word was God

Jn 1

WORD TO WORD

4

WORD TO WORD

Sometimes in the Psalms, David was in situations in which he was alone, betrayed, despairing, forlorn, hungry, mistreated, misunderstood, wounded, near death.

Sometimes it seemed he was a million miles away from being the king of Israel he was anointed to be. He made mistakes, his heart ruled his head at times, and he blew it in style!

Nevertheless, God saw something special in David's heart. David was a man who knew how to admit his sin – and repent. God likes that.

There were many times that David had to draw on his inner resources, and 'encourage himself in the Lord' when there was nothing and no-one else. He had learnt the hard way that God was faithful and had never deserted him.

David wrote many of the Psalms as hard evidence of a close relationship with God, nurtured through times of loneliness, stress, pressure.

174

When you're going through such trials and tests, do as the psalmist did. Take the Word of God and speak it, sing it, declare it – out loud. Speak to yourself in psalms, hymns, spiritual songs, scripture, as many times as is necessary for the truth and reality of it to invade and strengthen your spirit.

Here are a few simple Word-Prayers to start you off. Get into the habit and see how it transforms your day!

All Things Are Possible

All things are possible with God.

If I have faith that is like a grain of mustard seed, I can say to this mountain "MOVE" from here to there, and it *will* move and nothing shall be impossible to me.

Is anything too difficult for the Lord? The Lord can do all things and no thought or purpose of His can be restrained or thwarted.

By His promise and His oath it is impossible for God ever to prove false or deceive me if I have fled to Him for refuge and I have mighty indwelling strength and strong encouragement to grasp and hold fast to the hope appointed and set before me as an anchor for my soul.

His Word will not return void but will accomplish all it sets out to perform and He will bring every good work in me to completion.

God is able to make all grace abound to me in whatever circumstance I am in and His grace is sufficient, more than enough, for me.

He is able to guard and to keep me from falling and to present me blameless before the presence of His glory with exceeding joy.

The only thing that makes it impossible to please God is lack of faith (unbelief) in His Word. It is also impossible for God to lie.

All the promises of God are Yes and Amen in Christ Jesus.

"But thanks be to God Who *always* leads me in victory in Christ Jesus".

By His mighty power at work in me He is able to accomplish far more than I can ever hope, think or imagine!

POSSIBLE !

Food For Thought

I am a spirit. I have a soul and I live in a body. My body is the temple of the Holy Spirit. The Anointed One and His anointing dwells in me and my flesh is subject to the authority of God's Word. I am a good steward of this vessel and I present my body as a living sacrifice, acceptable to God. I am changed in my eating habits by the renewing of my mind, by changing the way I think. I do not concentrate on the flesh first, which is of self and selfish, but on the Spirit which is life and I feed myself on the Word of God, exercising self-control in all things.

I focus on every good word that proceeds out of the mouth of God, and I taste and see that the Lord is good. I have a body and a lifestyle which honours and pleases God and I exercise faith and give God thanks for everything I offer to my mouth, eating only at appointed meal-times and counting my food as holy and healthy to my body.

I discipline my body and take authority over slack and uncontrolled eating habits. Although everything is lawful for me, not everything is good for me and I choose not to abuse my body.

My food is to do the will of God and I feed and strengthen my spirit until it is stronger than my flesh concerning what and when I eat. I choose not to make an idol of my flesh.

I belong to Christ and I have nailed the passions and desires of my sinful nature to the Cross. I hunger and thirst for righteousness, not for more food. I am filled with the Holy Spirit, not more food. I get my teeth into the Word of God, not more food. I let heaven fill my thoughts, not more food fill my stomach.

I replace a bad habit with something good. I press on to victory. I am an over-comer and more than a conqueror in these things. I make progress every day, and one day at a time I exercise faith and I do what is pleasing to God, including what and how I eat.

I will be found faithful in this!

> *Whatever is the thing with which you may be struggling, find some scriptures that are relevant to it and turn them into a prayer confession, boldly declaring the truth and authority of God's Word. Speak to your mountain until you see it cast down into the ample depths of defeat.*

Get A Life!

Repeat after me. Ready? Go!

His mercies are new every morning. This is the day the Lord has made. I will rejoice and be glad in it. He sets before me LIFE and death, therefore I choose LIFE! I will not forget all His benefits towards me. I will read all of Psalm 103 and put my name in there and claim those promises as my own.

The thief comes to kill, rob and destroy but Jesus is come that I might have LIFE and have it abundantly! He is the Way, the Truth and the LIFE. I have a destiny, a purpose, a future, a plan to fulfil and I will LIVE it out! He suffered death ... that I might have LIFE. I have everything to live for. I have eternal LIFE in Christ Jesus. I do not look at the circumstances around me. I look at Him who sees and knows everything about me and is a good God who gives good gifts to His children.

Circumstances are subject to change, but He is the same yesterday, today and forever. There is no shadow of turning in Him. I will not turn to the right or to the left.

I will keep my eyes and my mind focussed and centred on Him and I will be kept in perfect peace. I will lift up my head so that the King of Glory may be seen by me.

Why are you downcast oh my soul? I will yet praise my God. I will encourage myself in the Lord. I will cast down every vain imagination because He is a God of faithfulness and no injustice. Good and upright is He. The Lover of my soul is He. My Shepherd. My Shelter. My Comfort. My strong Tower. A mighty Fortress is my God.

He's the A. He's the Z. Therefore He has my front and my back covered! His angels surround me to guard me in all my ways so I won't stumble or fall. He's my Provider. He's my Protector. My El Shaddai – the God Who is *more* than enough.

I will praise Him while I have LIFE and breath in my being and then – I will praise Him for all eternity.

Life!!

Joy Is On The Way

I will not be depressed. I will put on a garment of praise. I will rejoice in hope. I will give thanks at all times, for this is God's will concerning me. This is the day the Lord has made, I will rejoice and be glad in it. I will praise the Lord at all times, His praise shall continually be in my mouth. I will submit to the Lord and resist the devil, therefore he must flee away from me. I will rejoice in the Lord always; again I will say "Rejoice!" I claim the promises of God as my own and having done all, I stand in faith.

I don't allow what happens today to ruin my tomorrow. I don't allow the past to govern my future. I let go of fears, discouragements, disappointments, hurts – and move towards the good things that God has planned for my future.

The devil doesn't impress me, so he can't oppress me and therefore he won't depress me.

I think of whatsoever things are pure and lovely and of good report.

My burden is light and easy to be borne. I cast my cares on Him for He cares for me. Weeping may endure for a night but joy comes in the morning!

I'm OK and I'm on my way!

"A merry heart doeth good like medicine."

Sometimes when you're going through 'stuff' you have to pray 'declare prayers' – on purpose! You have to open your mouth and pray it anyway, you have to do it afraid, do it when you're hurting and it's the last thing you feel like doing, do it when you're sick, lonely, broke, whatever it is. Speak to the situation, speak to the principalities and powers, speak to God words of life and faith. Put God in remembrance of His Word and trust Him to act upon it.

This Is The Day

Ps 118 : 24

This is the day which the Lord has made; I will rejoice and be glad in it! "I will enjoy life on purpose and will not go by how I feel."

This is a stand-alone verse to quote at those times when your flesh has gone off in a direction all by itself. It is of special significance to me as when many years ago, I was having a particularly 'down-day', I remember my husband asking me for my bible. He flicked through it industriously for a while until he eventually 'plonked an open page' before me. Smiling triumphantly he pointed to the above verse, saying "read that!" as he calmly went off again about his business.

It had the desired effect. I was absolutely gob-smacked and have never forgotten the incident — or the verse!

Why so surprised? Wouldn't you be if your non-church attending, unbelieving-and-proud-of-it husband challenged you on a point of your own faith?

I give you My

WRD

In the beginning was the Word, and the Word was with God, and the Word was God

Jn 1

A WORD IN YOUR EAR

5

A WORD IN YOUR EAR

Here are a few reminders of the power that is packed into the Word of God, and how scripture reveals the very attributes and presence of the Word Himself – life, light, faith, knowledge, eternal, purity, truth, active, accurate, love, salvation, protection, healing, provision. You name it – He *is* it!

Hide the Word in your heart and He'll hide you in His.

I will make known My
words to you
Prov 1 : 23

Your word is a lamp to
my feet and a light to my
path
Ps119 : 105

The words that I have
spoken to you are spirit
and are life
Jn 6 : 63

In the beginning was the
Word, and the Word
was with God, and the
Word was God
Jn 1 : 1

He who hears my
Word, and believes
Him who sent Me has
eternal life
Jn 5 : 24

Faith comes by hearing
and hearing by the Word
of God
Rom 10 : 17

Forever, O Lord, Your word
is settled in heaven
Ps 119 : 89

The Word of our God
stands forever
Is 40 : 8

His Name is called the
Word of God
Rev 19 : 13

Be diligent to present
yourself approved to
God ... handling
accurately the word
of truth
2 Tim 2:15

Man shall live ... by
every word that
proceeds out of the
mouth of God
Mat 4:4

You are already clean
because of the word
which I have spoken to
you.
Jn 15:3

Be it done to me according
to your word
Lk 1:38

The word of God is living
and active and sharper
than any two-edged sword
Heb 4 : 12

Heaven and earth will pass
away, but My words will
not pass away
Mark 13:31

If you abide in My word, then
you are truly disciples of mine
Jn 15:7

..... You have words of
eternal life
Jn 6:68b

If anyone loves Me, he will keep My word
Jn 14 : 23

:And the Word became flesh and dwelt among us
Jn 1 : 14

The word of God is near you, in your mouth and in your heart … that if you confess with your mouth Jesus as Lord, and believe in your heart that God raised Him from the dead, you shall be saved
Rom 10:8a, 9

And Another Thing …

The Word Is Our
Fortress Of Faith

DOMINUS ILLUMINA TIO
MEA
God Is My Light

Put the Word First In Your
Life

When We Are Hidden In
Christ (The Word), Then Are
We Truly Revealed
Barbara Pavey

Keep God's Word And
God's Word Will Keep You

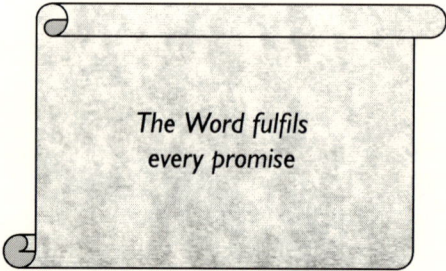

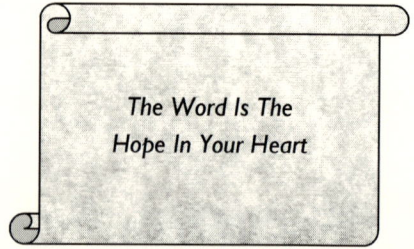

The Word Is The
Hope In Your Heart

The Word fulfils
every promise

The Word

Bless You

Ps 103 : 1-6, 8-22, 22b

Bless the Lord, O my soul; and all that is within me, bless His holy Name.

Bless the Lord, O my soul, and forget none of His benefits; Who pardons all your iniquities; Who heals all your diseases; Who redeems your life from the pit; Who crowns you with loving kindness and compassion; Who satisfies your years with good things, so that your things, so that your youth is renewed like the eagle.

The LORD performs righteous deeds, and judgements for all who are oppressed.

The LORD is compassionate and gracious, slow to anger and abounding in loving kindness.

He will not always strive with us; nor will He keep His anger forever. He has not dealt with us according to our sins, nor rewarded us according to our iniquities. For as high as the heavens are above the earth, so great is His loving kindness toward those who fear Him.

As far as the east is from the west, so far has He removed our transgressions from us.

Bless the LORD O my soul!

Bless You

Check it out – the whole of Ps 103 will bless you!

I Am

Genesis 22:14	Jehovah Jireh	The Lord my Provider
Exodus 15:26	Jehovah Ropheh	The Lord my Healer
Exodus 17:15	Jehovah Nissi	The Lord my Banner
Exodus 31:13	Jehovah Makedesh	The Lord my Sanctifier
Exodus 38:45	Jehovah Shammah	The God Who is There
Judges 6:24	Jehovah Shalom	The Lord my Peace
I Samuel 1:3	Jehovah Z'baoth	The Lord of Hosts
Psalms 7:17	Jehovah Elyon	The Lord Most High
Psalms 23:1	Jehovah Rohi	The Lord my Shepherd
Jeremiah 23:6	Jehovah T'Sidkenu	The Lord my Righteousness
Exodus 15:3		The Lord my Warrior

I AM

Safe In Your Arms

Ps 91

You who sit down in the High God's presence, spend the night in Shaddai's shadow, say this: "God, you're my refuge. I trust in you and I'm safe!"

That's right – He rescues you from hidden traps, shields you from deadly hazards.

His huge outstretched arms protect you – under them you're perfectly safe; His arms fend off all harm.

Fear nothing – not wild wolves in the night, not flying arrows in the day, not disease that erupts at high noon.

Even though others succumb all around, drop like flies right and left, no harm will even graze you.

You'll stand untouched, watch it all from a distance, watch the wicked turn into corpses.

Yes, because GOD'S your refuge, the High God your very own home, evil can't get close to you, harm can't get through the door.

He ordered His angels to guard you wherever you go.

If you stumble, they'll catch you; their job is to keep you from falling. You'll walk unharmed among lions and snakes, and kick young lions and serpents from the path.

"If you'll hold on to Me for dear life," says GOD, "I'll get you out of any trouble. I'll give you the best of care if you'll only get to know Me and trust Me. Call Me and I'll answer, be at your side in bad times; I'll rescue you, then throw a party. I'll give you a long life, give you a long drink of salvation!" (MSG)

safe

Word Power

WATCH YOUR TONGUE

Prov 25:11   "A word fitly spoken and in due season is like apples of gold in settings of silver." (Amp)

Mat 12:35   "A good person produces good words from a good heart, and an evil person produces evil words from an evil heart." (NLT)

Prov 18:21   "Words kill, words give life; they're either poison or fruit – you choose." (MSG)

1 Pet 3:10   "If you want a happy life and good days, keep your tongue from speaking evil, and keep your life from telling lies." (NLT)

Prov 19:1   "Smart people know how to hold their tongue; their grandeur is to forgive and forget." (MSG)

Phil 2:14-15 *"In everything you do, stay away from complaining and arguing, so no one can speak a word of blame against you."* (NLT)

Prov 15:1 *"A gentle answer turns away wrath, but a harsh words stirs up anger."*

Think before you speak

You've Got Me Covered

Ps 139 Verses 1 – 18 (AMP)

"O LORD, you have searched me (thoroughly) and have known me.

You know my down-sitting and my uprising; You understand my thought afar off.

You sift and search out my path and my lying down, and You are acquainted with all my ways.

For there is not a word in my tongue (still unuttered), but, behold O Lord, You know it altogether.

You have beset me and shut me in – behind and before, and You have laid Your hand upon me.

Your (infinite) knowledge is too wonderful for me; it is high above me, I cannot reach it.

Where could I go from Your Spirit?   Or where could I flee from Your presence?

If I ascend up into heaven, You are there; if I make my bed in Sheol (the place of the dead), behold, You are there.

If I take the wings of the morning or dwell in the uttermost parts of the sea,

Even there shall Your hand lead me, and Your right hand shall hold me.

If I say, Surely the darkness shall cover me and the night shall be (the only) light about me,

Even the darkness hides nothing from You, but the night shines as the day; the darkness and the light are both alike to You.

For You did form my inward parts; You did knit me together in my mother's womb.

I will confess and praise You for You are fearful and wonderful and for the awful wonder of my birth! Wonderful are Your works, and that my inner self knows right well.

My frame was not hidden from You when I was being formed in secret (and) intricately and curiously wrought (as if embroidered with various colours) in the depths of the earth (a region of darkness and mystery).

Your eyes saw my unformed substance, and in Your book all the days (of my life) were written before ever they took shape, when as yet there was none of them.

How precious and weighty also are Your thoughts to me, O God! How vast is the sum of them!

If I could count them, they would be more in number than the sand. When I awoke, (could I count to the end) I would still be with You."

See "I Know You" in The Spoken Word

I give you my WORD

In the beginning was the Word, and the Word was with God, and the Word was God

Jn 1

THE SPOKEN WORD

6

THE SPOKEN WORD

Communication is the very heart of God. He does it so well and in so many different ways.

As I prayed about the title of this book, I mulled over several possibilities, and then … it was as though a heavenly light went on, and a thought dropped 'kerplunk!' into my spirit … and **'I give you My Word'** was seeded.

At times, God wants to relay to you special 'now' directions, strategy, wisdom, revelation, encouragement. Mostly, He simply wants to 'talk' to you.

It doesn't always come via earthquakewindandfire.org, mostly through stillsmallvoice.com.

In other words, not *usually* audibly, but internally. Expect God to speak to *you*. What he says will *always* line up with His Word.

Be still … and know that He *is* God.

Cracked Pots Or Golden Vessels

You are so special to Me because you are honest and open with Me about what is going on in your heart. It's not that I don't know, but so many of My children are not real with Me or themselves. They are not truthful concerning the issues in their world and live so much of their time behind self-made masks. So much so that the image they try to project becomes so real to them that they lose their own identity. It's a lie of the devil, a deception, and a bondage.

Let Me show you what happens to a life that covers up what is really going on inside. I'll liken it to a building, or a container. You see, when a structure or a vessel has flaws in it, cracks start to appear - at first, small, insignificant, unnoticed by human eyes. Over a period of time, the effects of everyday pressures such as weak material, exposure to the elements, improper foundations, insufficient firings, all begin to take their toll. Pollution, muck and mould enter those cracks and crevices, opening them even further. The cracks may remain there for many a year and everything may appear to be fine on the outside. At some stage the damage *will* become apparent and obvious.

Attempts to hide it by gluing, cementing, painting or varnishing may fool others for a while, but the cracks are danger signs of flaws which require professional attention. There comes a time when pressure from external or internal sources will actually bring about the collapse of the entire building or vessel.

It is the same with your lives. There are things which you go through, extreme circumstances and situations that have caused a weakening of your 'structure.' Sometimes subsidence occurs. The ground beneath your feet literally gets taken away and your whole world collapses. That which you believed was a sure foundation and upon which you were building your hopes and dreams, caves in upon you, causing much damage and in some cases, the collapse of your faith.

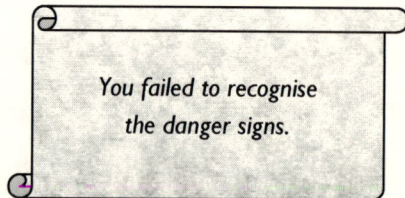

You failed to recognise the danger signs.

In many instances things are going on 'underground' as it were. Some of life's subsidence occurs through pain, grief, loss, rejection, misunderstanding, loneliness, despair, financial pressures, broken dreams. Sometimes as you try to get your house in order, you uncover some cracks.

Situations in your life that need dealing with but which have been pushed deep or glossed over because they are too painful for either yourself or others to face. Although you are bleeding inwardly, you stick a plaster over your mind and emotions and try to busy yourself with life. That plaster is called denial and it is masking dangerous poison and infection.

The things that are hidden will be uncovered. The things that are in darkness will be brought out into the Light. Deception will be exposed. There will eventually be nowhere to run and hide, because the pretence has to cease. Time when the masks of hypocrisy have to be removed and you face the Truth. I know that this is painful and uncomfortable because your mask has become your comforter but when you allow Me to come and open up the wounds I can be the Comforter Who comes alongside to help and to heal. I will do this anyway but I prefer to have your cooperation that we might work this through together.

The reason that this is necessary is because I never paper over cracks. I deal with Truth because I AM Truth. When I expose, it is not to shame, condemn, humiliate, but because I love you and came to set the captive free. I have a beautiful plan and a perfect idea of how to use the vessel I have created you to be, and an eternal viewpoint. I have a place and position of use for you built on the sure foundation of My Word.

I reveal the cracks, the disappointments, the flaws and failures not to break you because a bruised reed I will never crush. No, these things are exposed to the Light and the Truth. As you are opened up I set about removing the dirt, the pus, the shame, the guilt and I apply My healing balm, the love of the Master Craftsman, to reshape, remould, restore, rebuild your broken life.

I have begun a good work in you and I will complete and perfect it. My workmanship is good, timely and eternal. It will stand the test of time and there will be no fault in it. No errors. No mistakes. Unshakeable. You are a model of craftsmanship.

No more cover-ups. No limits. No shackles. This is My time for you to know that I am exposing you – for the world to see My glory reflected in you.

With everlasting Love,
Your Master Craftsman,
Father God

Hey You!

I'm here.

Deep to deep, soul to soul, heart to heart.

That's the way I work My plans,

Carefully shaping your life with My skilful hands.

When you're wading in the shallows

I'm forever drawing you deeper

Because that's where I am

And I want to show you such wonderful things.

You are covered, protected, by the span of My wings.

Out of your depth and into My care,

Watching over you constantly, never sleeping, just 'there.'

I want you to embrace every part of Me.

As I look at you, such a jewel I see.

I am the keeper of your soul

And I will never abandon you My little one.

I lead you, feed you, care for you

And always always I am there for you.

Precious, most precious in My sight

Are those with whom I walk in light.

And you, you contain a deposit of My grace,

You shine and My glory illumines your face.

Stand still in the eye of the storm

And watch Me, such wonders will I perform.

Trust My judgement, trust My Name

And know that I will never put you to shame.

You.

Special, priceless, called, chosen, unique.

You will move mountains as My words you speak,

Look up, awaken your faith, stir up each gift,

Strong one, look up as your head I lift.

You.

Warrior, priest, servant, friend,

You will live with me, age without end.

You in Me, eternally,

Me in you, such unity.

You.

I Know You

I know you.
Before there was ever a thought in your parent's minds,
I knew you.

I loved you before you were knit together.
I had you in my heart and I simply had to find
A channel through which to produce you.
I entrusted the care of you into human hands.
I took that chance.
I put the preciousness of all that is you into human form
And I have watched over you all these years.
I know you.

I have never, not for one second, forsaken you
And as you reached that moment when you entrusted
Your life back to me, my joy was complete.
I know you.

There is no-one like you in my eyes.
The special-ness of you shines in a world of darkness.
You are My rare jewel, My priceless treasure.
My heart is soft towards you.

With tenderness I hold you to Me, gently, for a bruised
reed I will not crush.
I am restoring you, renewing, remoulding.
Fear Me not.
Come, let us walk again in closeness.
I know you.

I know you with a thoroughness, a completeness,
A confidence which says I *will* finish
All that I purpose for you.
I know you.

Utterly and intimately,
And in the knowing will I perform
All that is right for you.
I know you.

I
KNOW
YOU

This was written for someone who needed to know that life was not in vain and without meaning or purpose. Written for one whom God says is special and precious.

My own experience is that I am one of twins, yet there were no scanning machines at the time of my birth. My mother did not know she was carrying two babies and after the delivery of the first one, she was about to be stitched up ... but the midwife noticed there was still a bump! There I was, maybe a shock, maybe a surprise to my parents ... but not to God.

God made no mistake with you either – and this is equal confirmation for you that your unique life is a rare jewel in the hands of a loving heavenly Father.

Use your life and the talents He has given you in a way that blesses others and glorifies Him.

212

New Day

Today is a new day, a new way to know My love

I'm breaking up your fallow ground, watering from above.

My mercy's new as each dawn breaks and through each trial and test

You'll find a new anointing, experience peace and rest.

I am the Shepherd of your soul, the One who'll guide and lead.

It's My responsibility My sheep to daily feed.

I know the plans I have for you, they're not to cause you harm,

And as you learn to praise Me more, you'll hear My voice as balm.

The pressures that you often bear I don't require of you.

My yoke is easy for I take the strain of all you do.

Yet sometimes I *will* stretch you, I'll cause you to know need,

For it's then that you will run to Me and find Me God indeed.

I want to cause new growth in you, a growth in holiness.

In you My character I'll build, overlay My righteousness.

It's a time for stepping out, in trust and faith you'll prove.

It's a time to cast aside all doubt, for I'm about to move.

Know Me as the God of grace, spend time alone with Me,

See the love upon My face, come close and you will see.

Don't ever think I got it wrong when the choice of you I made,

And know that I am making strong, though answers seem delayed.

For I have spoken blessing, and I have truly heard

And it shall surely come to pass, according to My Word,

So set your face to follow Me, don't limit or restrict,

My timing isn't yours to guess at or predict.

Let go of all your preconceived conditions, thoughts, ideas

Just come – and find My perfect rest. Trust me in your tears.

Your worship is important, and in it's constancy

Releases in the Spirit faith and hope in Me.

And hope will have its perfect way.

Faith is victory's seed,

And those who truly know their God

Are those who will succeed!

(Prophetic Poem)

The Strongest Love

Your life's lived independently with little thought of Me.

Self-contained and self-assured you always are,

But I'll never stop reaching out to you, I gave My life you see,

From a distance I am calling you, watching from afar.

You've tried to make it on your own,

Never-stop-trying one, high-flying one.

Thought you'd go it all alone.

I know – but you came undone.

It never worked out the way you thought,

Broken dreams,

That's the way it seems,

In our own web we're sometimes caught

But see, My love-light beams.

One day, one day you'll have to choose,

One day you'll know that I believe in you.

Give Me your life, what have you got to lose?

I'll free you from within and I'll never leave you.

Strong love, the deepest ocean can't contain,

For without Me you just won't make it.

Strong love that offers hope again,

Strong love, it's free if you will take it.

Haven't you room for Me?

Won't you open your eyes?

Won't you look and see

When you're reaching for the skies?

There's One Who died for you,

Poured out His precious blood,

One whose way is true.

My Name is Jesus.

Won't you take hold of My strong Love?

Song of Songs 8:6-7 "For love is as strong as death. Many waters cannot quench love."

I give you my

WORD

Jn 1

In the beginning was the Word, and the Word was with God, and the Word was God

THE LAST WORD

7

THE LAST WORD

"For I *so* loved *you*, that I gave *everything* to get you. I'm the First Word and the Last Word."

"Let me be the Forever Word in *your* heart."

Father God.

Coming Home

Here's a prayer for you, if, as you've read through these pages, you've realised that you have perhaps drifted away from the Lord and now want to come close again.

'Father God,

It's me again. You know I've been running and resisting, putting up barriers and wearing masks, convincing myself that I don't need You in my life.

You know I've kept busy so I don't have to think about the ache and the void in my heart.

Well, it's rubber-hits-the-road time, and I just want to say 'I'm sorry.'

Will you, as You hold out your hand of grace to this prodigal, restore me in my relationship with You?

Forgive me for doing it 'my way' – it hasn't worked, and thank You that Your mercy is new to me every day. I sure need it.

Amen.'

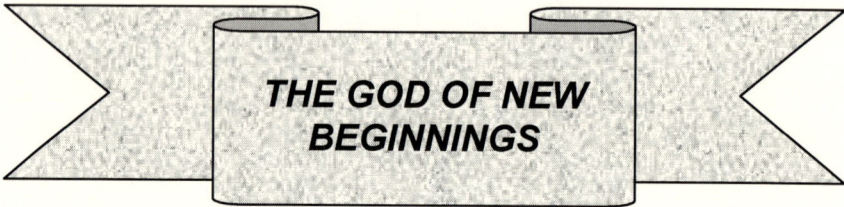

THE GOD OF NEW BEGINNINGS

How To Be Born Again

I am the way, and the truth, and the life; no one comes to the Father but through Me (Jn 14:6).

I am the door; if anyone enters through Me, he shall be saved (Jn 10:9).

If you confess with your mouth Jesus as Lord, and believe in your heart that God raised Him from the dead, you shall be saved (Rom 10:9).

As many as receive Me, I give the right to become children of God, even to those who believe in My name (Jn 1:12).

If you confess your sins, I am faithful and just to forgive your sins and to cleanse you from all unrighteousness (1 Jn 1:9).

At the name of Jesus, every knee should bow ... and every tongue confess that Jesus is Lord, to the glory of God the Father (Phil 2:10-11).

You have been bought with a price (1 Cor 6:20).

Without the shedding of blood there is no forgiveness (Heb 9:22).

Behold, the Lamb of God who takes away the sin of the world (Jn 1:29).

For God so loved the world, that He gave His only begotten Son, that whoever believes in Him should not perish, but have eternal life (Jn 3:16).

For the wages of sin is death, but the free gift of God is eternal life in Christ Jesus our Lord (Rom 6:23)

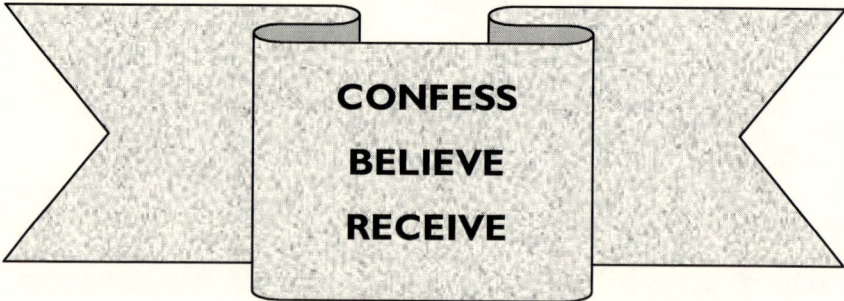

CONFESS

BELIEVE

RECEIVE

The Last Word

This book is written to bless, encourage and perhaps sometimes to challenge your thinking.

Here's a prayer for those that may not yet have the personal relationship with God that the Bible terms 'being born again' (see *Jn 3:3, 5-7*).

> 'Lord Jesus Christ,
> Thank You for watching over me all these years,
> But now I admit I've sinned and gone my own way,
> And I know I need Your forgiveness.
>
> I want to turn my life over to You
> And I want You to be number One in it.
>
> Thank You for dying on the Cross to take away my sins,
> And for washing them away with Your blood.

Thank You for being willing to wipe my slate clean
And give me a whole new life in You.
I ask You to come into my life by Your Holy Spirit
And fill me with Yourself.

Be my Lord and my Friend forever.

Thank You Lord Jesus,
Amen.'

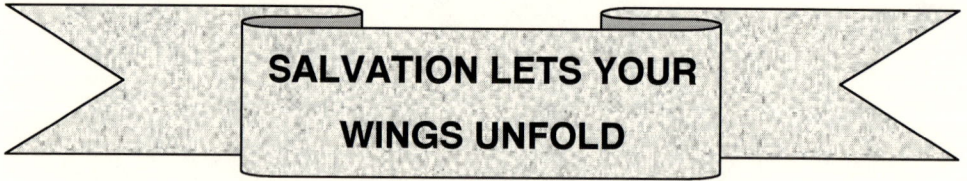

SALVATION LETS YOUR WINGS UNFOLD

Turn to me and be saved,
all the ends of the earth!
For I am God,
and there is no other.
Isaiah 45:22

To contact the Author visit www.igiveyoumyword.com

see Author Notes overleaf

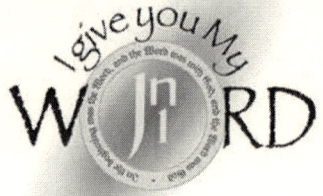

About The Author

I'm **Barbara Pavey**, born and brought up in West London, with a brother who shared womb-time with me, my 10-minute older twin!

An Accountant by trade, I'm keen on languages, travel, garden and home design (with hubby), cooking, reading and learning, and enjoying new experiences – this book being one of them!

I was born-again at the age of 12, in a Youth Group at the local Baptist Church and have always had a heart for short-term mission trips. As a keen bible scholar and teacher I have been privileged to minister in Malaysia, Spain and still frequently in Serbia amongst a growing network of evangelical churches. In UK, I have spoken at Youth meetings, local churches and in Ladies' Ministry. God has also gifted me administratively and I have helped organise many social events.

My Christian faith has always been my spiritual anchor and my bible the plumb-line by which I live life. This faith has to be worked out daily. I've drifted many times but that anchor is connected to Jesus the Rock – and He has never left me! Because of Him – I'm still here!